Illustrator CS3
Basic

Instructor's Edition

ACE Edition

Illustrator CS3: Basic

President & Chief Executive Officer:	Michael Springer
Vice President, Product Development:	Adam A. Wilcox
Vice President, Operations:	Josh Pincus
Director of Publishing Systems Development:	Dan Quackenbush
Writer:	Dave Fink
Developmental Editor:	Don Tremblay
Series Designer:	Adam A. Wilcox

Trademarks

ILT Series is a trademark of Axzo Press.

Some of the product names and company names used in this book have been used for identification purposes only and may be trademarks or registered trademarks of their respective manufacturers and sellers.

Disclaimers

We reserve the right to revise this publication and make changes from time to time in its content without notice.

The Adobe Approved Certification Courseware logo is either a registered trademark or trademark of Adobe Systems Incorporated in the United States and/or other countries. The Adobe Approved Certification Courseware logo is a proprietary trademark of Adobe. All rights reserved.

The ILT Series is independent from ProCert Labs, LLC and Adobe Systems Incorporated, and are not affiliated with ProCert Labs and Adobe in any manner. This publication may assist students to prepare for an Adobe Certified Expert exam, however, neither ProCert Labs nor Adobe warrant that use of this material will ensure success in connection with any exam.

ISBN 10: 1-4260-9485-X
ISBN 13: 978-1-4260-9485-9

Printed in the United States of America

1 2 3 4 5 6 7 8 9 10 GL 10 09 08

Contents

Introduction

After reading this introduction, you will know how to:

A Use ILT Series manuals in general.

B Use prerequisites, a target student description, course objectives, and a skills inventory to properly set students' expectations for the course.

C Set up a classroom to teach this course.

D Get support for setting up and teaching this course.

Topic A: About the manual

ILT Series philosophy

Our goal is to make you, the instructor, as successful as possible. To that end, our manuals facilitate students' learning by providing structured interaction with the software itself. While we provide text to help you explain difficult concepts, the hands-on activities are the focus of our courses. Leading the students through these activities will teach the skills and concepts effectively.

We believe strongly in the instructor-led class. For many students, having a thinking, feeling instructor in front of them will always be the most comfortable way to learn. Because the students' focus should be on you, our manuals are designed and written to facilitate your interaction with the students, and not to call attention to manuals themselves.

We believe in the basic approach of setting expectations, then teaching, and providing summary and review afterwards. For this reason, lessons begin with objectives and end with summaries. We also provide overall course objectives and a course summary to provide both an introduction to and closure on the entire course.

Our goal is your success. We encourage your feedback in helping us to continually improve our manuals to meet your needs.

Manual components

The manuals contain these major components:

- Table of contents
- Introduction
- Units
- Appendix
- Course summary
- Quick reference
- Glossary
- Index

Each element is described below.

Table of contents

The table of contents acts as a learning roadmap for you and the students.

Introduction

The introduction contains information about our training philosophy and our manual components, features, and conventions. It contains target student, prerequisite, objective, and setup information for the specific course. Finally, the introduction contains support information.

Units

Units are the largest structural component of the actual course content. A unit begins with a title page that lists objectives for each major subdivision, or topic, within the unit. Within each topic, conceptual and explanatory information alternates with hands-on activities. Units conclude with a summary comprising one paragraph for each topic, and an independent practice activity that gives students an opportunity to practice the skills they've learned.

The conceptual information takes the form of text paragraphs, exhibits, lists, and tables. The activities are structured in two columns, one telling students what to do, the other providing explanations, descriptions, and graphics. Throughout a unit, instructor notes are found in the left margin.

Appendix

The appendix for this course lists the Adobe Certified Expert (ACE) exam objectives for Illustrator CS3 along with references to corresponding coverage in Course ILT courseware.

Course summary

This section provides a text summary of the entire course. It is useful for providing closure at the end of the course. The course summary also indicates the next course in this series, if there is one, and lists additional resources students might find useful as they continue to learn about the software.

Quick reference

The quick reference is an at-a-glance job aid summarizing some of the more common features of the software.

Glossary

The glossary provides definitions for all of the key terms used in this course.

Index

The index at the end of this manual makes it easy for you and your students to find information about a particular software component, feature, or concept.

Manual conventions

We've tried to keep the number of elements and the types of formatting to a minimum in the manuals. We think this aids in clarity and makes the manuals more classically elegant looking. But there are some conventions and icons you should know about.

	Item	Description
Instructor note/icon	*Italic text*	In conceptual text, indicates a new term or feature.
	Bold text	In unit summaries, indicates a key term or concept. In an independent practice activity, indicates an explicit item that you select, choose, or type.
	`Code font`	Indicates code or syntax.

	`Longer strings of ▶`
	`   code will look ▶`
	`   like this.`
		In the hands-on activities, any code that's too long to fit on a single line is divided into segments by one or more continuation characters (▶). This code should be entered as a continuous string of text.

Instructor notes.		In the left margin, provide tips, hints, and warnings for the instructor.
	Select **bold item**	In the left column of hands-on activities, bold sans-serif text indicates an explicit item that you select, choose, or type.
	Keycaps like (↵ ENTER)	Indicate a key on the keyboard you must press.
⚠ *Warning icon.*		Warnings prepare instructors for potential classroom management problems.
✔ *Tip icon.*		Tips give extra information the instructor can share with students.
Setup icon.		Setup notes provide a realistic business context for instructors to share with students, or indicate additional setup steps required for the current activity.
Projector icon.		Projector notes indicate that there is a PowerPoint slide for the adjacent content.

Hands-on activities

The hands-on activities are the most important parts of our manuals. They are divided into two primary columns. The "Here's how" column gives short directions to the students. The "Here's why" column provides explanations, graphics, and clarifications. To the left, instructor notes provide tips, warnings, setups, and other information for the instructor only. Here's a sample:

Do it!

A-1: Creating a commission formula

Take the time to make sure your students understand this worksheet. We'll be here a while.

Here's how	Here's why
1 Open Sales	This is an oversimplified sales compensation worksheet. It shows sales totals, commissions, and incentives for five sales reps.
2 Observe the contents of cell F4	F4 ▼ = =E4*C_Rate
	The commission rate formulas use the name "C_Rate" instead of a value for the commission rate.

For these activities, we have provided a collection of data files designed to help students learn each skill in a real-world business context. As students work through the activities, they will modify and update these files. Of course, students might make a mistake and therefore want to re-key the activity starting from scratch. To make it easy to start over, students will rename each data file at the end of the first activity in which the file is modified. Our convention for renaming files is to add the word "My" to the beginning of the file name. In the above activity, for example, students are using a file called "Sales" for the first time. At the end of this activity, they would save the file as "My sales," thus leaving the "Sales" file unchanged. If students make mistakes, they can start over using the original "Sales" file.

In some activities, however, it might not be practical to rename the data file. Such exceptions are indicated with an instructor note. If students want to retry one of these activities, you will need to provide a fresh copy of the original data file.

PowerPoint presentations

Each unit in this course has an accompanying PowerPoint presentation. These slide shows are designed to support your classroom instruction while providing students with a visual focus. Each presentation begins with a list of unit objectives and ends with a unit summary slide. We strongly recommend that you run these presentations from the instructor's station as you teach this course. A copy of PowerPoint Viewer is included, so it is not necessary to have PowerPoint installed on your computer.

The ILT Series PowerPoint add-in

The CD also contains a PowerPoint add-in that enables you to do two things:

- Create slide notes for the class
- Display a control panel for the Flash movies embedded in the presentations

To load the PowerPoint add-in:

1   Copy the Course_ILT.ppa file to a convenient location on your hard drive.
2   Start PowerPoint.
3   Choose Tools, Macro, Security to open the Security dialog box. On the Security Level tab, select Medium (if necessary), and then click OK.
4   Choose Tools, Add-Ins to open the Add-Ins dialog box. Then, click Add New.
5   Browse to and select the Course_ILT.ppa file, and then click OK. A message box will appear, warning you that macros can contain viruses.
6   Click Enable Macros. The Course_ILT add-in should now appear in the Available Add-Ins list (in the Add-Ins dialog box). The "x" in front of Course_ILT indicates that the add-in is loaded.
7   Click Close to close the Add-Ins dialog box.

After you complete this procedure, a new toolbar will be available at the top of the PowerPoint window. This toolbar contains a single button labeled "Create SlideNotes." Click this button to generate slide-notes files in both text (.txt) and Excel (.xls) format. By default, these files will be saved to the folder that contains the presentation. If the PowerPoint file is on a CD-ROM or in some other location to which the slide-notes files cannot be saved, you will be prompted to save the presentation to your hard drive and try again.

When you run a presentation and come to a slide that contains a Flash movie, you will see a small control panel in the lower-left corner of the screen. You can use this panel to start, stop, and rewind the movie, or to play it again.

Topic B: Setting student expectations

Properly setting students' expectations is essential to your success. This topic will help you do that by providing:

- Prerequisites for this course
- A description of the target student
- A list of the objectives for the course
- A skills assessment for the course

Course prerequisites

Students taking this course should be familiar with personal computers and the use of a keyboard and a mouse. Furthermore, this course assumes that students have completed the following courses or have equivalent experience:

- *Windows XP: Basic*

Target student

This course is designed for anyone who wants to learn the basics of using Illustrator CS3 to create graphics for use in print, or in other media. Students will get the most out of this course if their goal is to become proficient in using Illustrator CS3 to create simple and complex shapes, add color and text to illustrations, and modify and group items in illustrations.

Adobe ACE certification

This course is also designed to help your students pass the Adobe Certified Expert (ACE) exam for Illustrator CS3. For complete certification training, students should complete this course and *Illustrator CS3: Advanced, ACE Edition*.

Course objectives

You should share these overall course objectives with your students at the beginning of the day. This will give the students an idea about what to expect, and it will help you identify students who might be misplaced. Students are considered misplaced when they lack the prerequisite knowledge or when they already know most of the subject matter to be covered.

Note: In addition the general objectives listed below, specific ACE exam objectives are listed at the beginning of each topic and highlighted by instructor notes throughout each unit. For a complete mapping of ACE objectives to the ILT Series content, see Appendix A.

After completing this course, students will know how to:

- Start Illustrator and explore the Illustrator environment, navigate an Illustrator document, and use the Adobe Help Viewer.

- Create and save a new document, draw basic shapes, manipulate basic shapes to make complex shapes, and export an illustration.

- Adjust fill and stroke colors for shapes, adjust basic stroke options, and use the Eyedropper tool to sample colors.

- Embed raster images in an Illustrator document for the purpose of tracing them, draw shapes and paths by using the Pencil tool and the Pen tool, and select and edit paths.

- Use text tools to insert text into illustrations, manipulate text, and convert type to outlined shapes.

- Create new layers and organize them in the Layers panel, and manipulate layers by renaming layers, duplicating layers, and deleting layers.

- Import swatch libraries, open preset swatch libraries, export a swatch library, create and adjust gradients, and adjust transparency for items.

- Flow type through linked type containers and wrap text around items, set and format tabs, insert typographic characters, use character and paragraph styles, check spelling, find and replace text in a document, and manage fonts.

Skills inventory

Use the following form to gauge students' skill levels entering the class (students have copies in the introductions of their student manuals). For each skill listed, have students rate their familiarity from 1 to 5, with five being the most familiar. Emphasize that this is not a test. Rather, it is intended to provide students with an idea of where they're starting from at the beginning of class. If a student is wholly unfamiliar with all the skills, he or she might not be ready for the class. A student who seems to understand all of the skills, on the other hand, might need to move on to the next course in the series.

Skill	1	2	3	4	5
Exploring the Illustrator interface					
Identifying Illustrator tools and panels					
Managing files with Adobe Bridge					
Using the Navigation tools					
Using Help					
Creating a new document					
Changing document setup					
Creating basic shapes					
Drawing shapes precisely					
Selecting and scaling shapes					
Duplicating shapes					
Aligning and distributing shapes					
Using the Add to Shape Area command					
Grouping shapes					
Rotating shapes					
Adjusting stacking order					
Adding metadata					
Exporting an illustration					
Using the Swatches panel					
Using the Color panel					
Storing colors					

Skill	1	2	3	4	5
Setting basic stroke attributes					
Creating a dashed line					
Using the Eyedropper tool					
Importing a raster image					
Using the Pencil and Smooth tools					
Using the Pen tool					
Creating complex paths					
Editing anchor points					
Joining paths by using the Average and Join commands					
Cutting paths by using the Scissors tool					
Adding text					
Importing text					
Using the Area Type tool					
Positioning type on a path					
Converting text to outlines					
Creating a new layer					
Changing layer stacking order					
Hiding and locking layers					
Organizing sublayers					
Duplicating a layer					
Importing swatches from other documents					
Adding swatches from a spot color library					
Saving a swatch library					
Creating a new gradient					
Adjusting a gradient					
Setting transparency					

Skill	1	2	3	4	5
Linking type containers					
Wrapping text around objects					
Setting tabs					
Inserting typographic characters					
Using character styles					
Using paragraph styles					
Checking spelling					
Finding and replacing text					
Managing font usage					

Topic C: Classroom setup

All our courses assume that each student has a personal computer to use during the class. Our hands-on approach to learning requires they do. This topic gives information on how to set up the classroom to teach this course. It includes minimum requirements for the students' personal computers, setup information for the first time you teach the class, and setup information for each time that you teach after the first time you set up the classroom.

Hardware requirements

Each student's personal computer should have:

- A keyboard and a mouse
- Intel Pentium 4, Intel Centrino, Intel Xeon, or Intel Core Duo (or compatible) processor
- 512MB of RAM (1GB recommended)
- At least 2.5GB of available hard-disk space for installation
- A DVD-ROM drive
- An XGA monitor with support for at least 1024x768 resolution and at least 24-bit color

Software requirements

You will need the following software:

- Microsoft Windows XP with Service Pack 2 or Windows Vista Home Premium, Business, Ultimate, or Enterprise (certified for 32-bit editions)
- Adobe Illustrator CS3

Network requirements

The following network components and connectivity are also required for this course:

- Internet access, for the following purposes:
    - Downloading the latest critical updates and service packs from www.windowsupdate.com
    - Downloading the Student Data files (if necessary)

First-time setup instructions

The first time you teach this course, you will need to perform the following steps to set up each student computer.

1 Install Windows XP on an NTFS partition according to the software manufacturer's instructions. If the student machines have Internet access, and they are behind a software or hardware firewall, install the latest critical updates and service packs from www.windowsupdate.com.

OR

Install Windows Vista according to the software manufacturer's instructions.

Note: You can also use Windows Vista, although the screen shots in this course were taken using Windows XP, so students' screens might look somewhat different. Also, some of the following setup instructions might differ slightly.

2 From the Control Panel, open the Display Properties dialog box and apply the following settings:

- Theme—Windows XP
- Screen resolution—1024 by 768 pixels
- Color quality—High (24 bit) or higher

3 Install Adobe Illustrator CS3 according to the software manufacturer's instructions. If you have the full version of Creative Suite 3, you need to install only Illustrator CS3 for this course.

a On the Installation Options screen, from the Install list, choose Selected Components.

b Clear all check boxes except the one for Adobe Illustrator CS3.

c Continue with the default installation. When asked whether to download updates, click Yes.

4 If you don't have the data CD that came with this manual, download the Student Data files for the course. You can download the data directly to student machines, to a central location on your own network, or to a disk.

a Connect to www.axzopress.com.

b Under Downloads, click Instructor-Led Training.

c Browse the subject categories to locate your course. Then click the course title to display a list of available downloads. (You can also access these downloads through our Catalog listings.)

d Click the link(s) for downloading the Student Data files, and follow the instructions that appear on your screen.

Setup instructions for every class

Every time you teach this course (including the first time), you will need to perform the following steps to set up each student computer.

1   Reset the workspace back to its original configuration. To do this, start Illustrator and choose Window, Workspace, [Basic].

2   Remove Outlander Color library from the Swatches folder within the Documents and Settings folder. Navigate to C:\Documents and Settings\[Current User]\Application Data\Adobe\Adobe Illustrator CS3 Settings\Swatches and delete the Outlander colors.ai document.

3   Delete the contents of the Student Data folder, if necessary. (If this is the first time you are teaching the course, create a folder named Student Data at the root of the hard drive. For a standard hard drive setup, this will be C:\Student Data.)

4   Copy the data files to the Student Data folder. (See the download instructions in the preceding section.)

CertBlaster exam preparation for ACE certification

CertBlaster pre- and post-assessment software is available for this course. To download and install this free software, students should complete the following steps:

1   Go to www.axzopress.com.

2   Under Downloads, click CertBlaster.

3   Click the link for Illustrator CS3.

4   Save the .EXE file to a folder on your hard drive. (**Note**: If you skip this step, the CertBlaster software will not install correctly.)

5   Click Start and choose Run.

6   Click Browse and then navigate to the folder that contains the .EXE file.

7   Select the .EXE file and click Open.

8   Click OK and follow the on-screen instructions. When prompted for the password, enter **c_illcs3**.

Topic D: Support

Your success is our primary concern. If you need help setting up this class or teaching a particular unit, topic, or activity, please don't hesitate to get in touch with us.

Contacting us

Please contact us through our Web site, www.axzopress.com. You will need to provide the name of the course, and be as specific as possible about the kind of help you need.

Instructor's tools

Our Web site provides several instructor's tools for each course, including course outlines and answers to frequently asked questions. To download these files, go to www.axzopress.com. Then, under Downloads, click Instructor-Led Training and browse our subject categories.

Unit 1

Getting started

Unit time: 50 minutes

Complete this unit, and you'll know how to:

A Start Illustrator and identify components of the Adobe Illustrator CS3 environment.

B Use views to change how objects appear in illustrations, and magnify and use the navigation tools to move and zoom in and out of illustrations.

C Use Adobe Help Viewer.

Topic A: The Illustrator environment

This topic covers the following ACE exam objectives for Illustrator CS3.

#	Objective
1.1	Describe the different components of the work area. (Components include: Artboard, Page area, Panels, and Tools.)
6.1	List and describe the functionality Adobe Bridge provides for viewing assets.

About Illustrator

Explanation

Adobe Illustrator CS3 is a graphics package used for creating illustrations, technical drawings, logos, Web graphics, and so on. The difference between Illustrator and some other types of graphic applications (such as Photoshop) is that it creates primarily vector-based artwork.

Vector artwork and raster images

Vector artwork consists of lines and curves that are defined by mathematical objects called vectors. You can alter the size of vector artwork without making the edges rough or jagged, as shown in the example in Exhibit 1-1. Sharp images, such as logos, that need smooth and precise edges are usually created as vector artwork, and then possibly exported as raster images depending on how they're used.

Raster images are composed of a grid, or raster, of small squares called pixels. Although they sometimes might appear similar to vector artwork, raster images are set at a fixed resolution. If you enlarge a raster image large enough, you can see individual pixels.

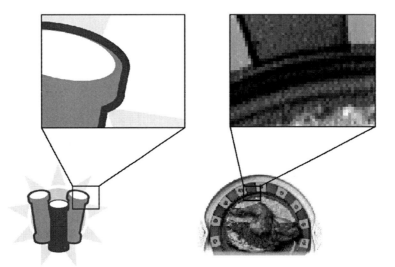

Exhibit 1-1: A magnified vector graphic (left) and raster image (right)

Starting Illustrator

To start Illustrator and open a document:

1   Choose Start, All Programs, Adobe Illustrator CS3.

2   The Welcome Screen appears, as shown in Exhibit 1-2.

3   Check Don't show again. This will prevent the screen from appearing each time the software starts.

4   Click Open to access an existing document, or click New Document to create a new document.

5   For an existing document, browse to the correct folder and open the document.

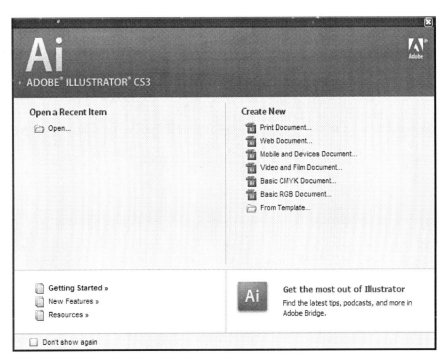

Exhibit 1-2: The Welcome Screen

Illustrator window components

ACE objective 1.1

The default interface elements are the *Tools panel*, the *Control panel*, the *artboard*, the *scratch area*, the default *panels*, the *Status bar*, and the *Zoom box*, as shown in Exhibit 1-3.

Tools panel   Control panel   Scratch area   Artboard

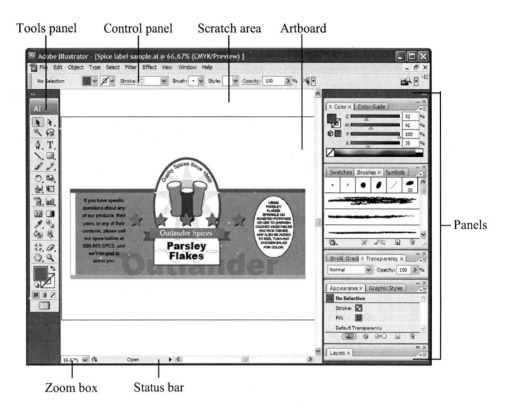

Panels

Zoom box   Status bar

Exhibit 1-3: The Illustrator application window

The following table describes the interface elements.

ACE objective 1.1

Item	Description
Tools panel	Contains button-like tools, which you can use to create, select, and modify items.
Control panel	Offers quick access to options related to the items you select. For example, when you select text, the Control panel displays text-formatting options such as type color, type style, type size, and alignment settings.
Artboard	Represents the maximum printable area. It is the solid rectangle in the center of the scratch area. You can set the size of the artboard each time you create a new drawing. However, the artboard might not match the page dimensions. For example, the artboard might be 15 x 20 inches, whereas the page dimensions are 8 1/2 x 11 inches.
Scratch area	Represents the area outside the artboard. You can use the scratch area for rough work. For example, you can create, edit, and store artwork on the scratch area before positioning it on the artboard. The artwork you create in the scratch area does not print with the illustration but is stored in the document.
Panels	Contain options you can use to select and apply colors, create and modify lines, rotate and shape images, and apply special effects. You can view or hide panels by selecting options from the Window menu.

Item	Description
Status bar	Displays information about the current tool in use, the date and time, the amount of virtual memory available for the open file, the number of times you can undo and redo, and the document color profile. To specify the type of information to display, select from the shortcut menu.
Zoom box	Displays the current magnification of the drawing relative to its actual size. You can change the magnification by either selecting a magnification level from the shortcut list or entering a value in the box.

The panel dock

By default, some panels are available in the panel dock on the right side of the work area. When the dock is collapsed, icons for the panels are visible. To expand the entire dock, click the Expand Dock button at the top-right of the dock. Alternatively, you can click individual icons to show only the desired panel.

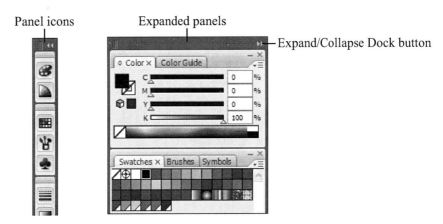

Exhibit 1-4: The collapsed panel dock (left) and expanded panel dock (right)

Whether the panel dock is expanded or collapsed, the panels are grouped based on their purpose. For example, the Color and Color Guide panels both have options for creating custom colors, so they are grouped, as shown in Exhibit 1-5. To switch panels, either click the icon you want in the collapsed panel dock, or click the panel tab in the expanded panel group.

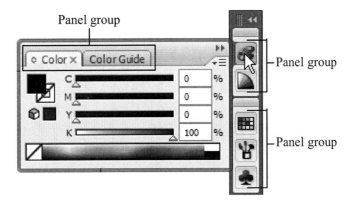

Exhibit 1-5: An example of a panel group

Do it!

A-1:   **Exploring the Illustrator interface**

Here's how	Here's why
1 Choose **Start**, **All Programs**, **Adobe Illustrator CS3**	To start Illustrator. The Adobe Illustrator CS3 Welcome Screen appears.
2 In the lower-left corner, check **Don't show again**	This will keep the screen from appearing each time you start Illustrator.
3 Click **Open...**	To open the Open dialog box.
4 Navigate to the current unit folder	
5 Select the **Spice label sample** document	
Click **Open**	You see an illustration of a spice label.
6 Maximize the document window	If necessary.
7 Observe the Tools panel	It is a docked panel on the left side of the work area and contains tools used to create, select, and modify artwork.
8 Observe the panel dock on the right side of the work area	By default, the panels in the dock are collapsed.
9 At the top of the panel dock, click the Expand Dock button, as shown	
	To expand the panels. Panels help you to monitor, arrange, and modify artwork, and you can view or hide them using the Window menu.
10 At the top of the panel dock, click the Collapse to Icons button	To collapse the panels so that only the icons are showing again.

ACE objective 1.1

If you want to access the Welcome Screen later, choose Help, Welcome Screen.

Help students to locate the current unit folder.

TIPS *You can also double-click the file to open it.*

Point out to students the basic components of the Illustrator window.

11   In the panel dock, click

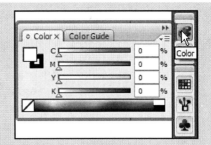

To expand just the Color and Color Guide panel group.

Click the Color icon again

To collapse the panel group.

12   Observe the Status bar

It is a small bar in the lower-left corner of the work area. It contains a shortcut menu and a Zoom box.

Click the shortcut menu

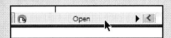

You can choose any option to view its related information.

13   Click on a blank area of the artboard

To close the menu.

14   In the Status bar, observe the Zoom box

The Zoom box shows the magnification of the artwork relative to its actual size.

Depending on the resolution of student screens, zoom percentages might differ from examples in this unit.

Click the arrow in the Zoom box, as shown

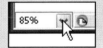

To expand the magnification list. You can select any value from this list to change the magnification.

15   Click on a blank area of the artboard

To close the Zoom list.

Illustrator panels

Explanation

ACE objective 1.1

To convert a docked panel to a floating panel, drag the panel tab anywhere in the work area. To float a panel group, drag a blank area just above or to the right of the tabs. If you want to keep several floating panel windows together, you can dock the panels one below the other. To do this, drag one floating panel or panel group to the bottom of another floating panel until a blue bar is visible, then release the mouse button. To move the docked floating panels, drag the top panel or panel group.

Panel display options

Panels also contain panel menus (shown in Exhibit 1-6), which include options in addition to the ones already visible on the panel. To display a panel menu, point to the small panel menu icon in the upper-right corner of the panel and press and hold the mouse button.

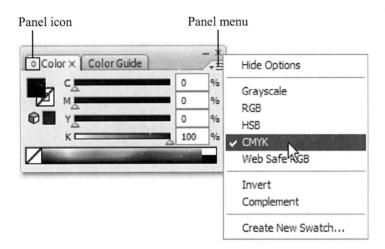

Exhibit 1-6: An example of a panel menu

Some panels can display two or three sets of options to let you control the amount of screen space the panel uses. If a panel tab displays an icon to the left of the tab name, like the icon in the Color tab in Exhibit 1-6, you can click the icon to switch views. You can also double-click the tab title to perform the same action.

You can resize panels to avoid cluttering the screen. To do so, either drag the lower-right corner of the panel or click the minimize/maximize button.

To view or hide panels, choose a panel from the Window menu. You can temporarily hide all panels with or without the Tools panel to view the artwork without any clutter:

- To hide all the open panels, including the Tools panel, press Tab.
- To display the hidden panels, press Tab again.
- To hide or show just the panel dock on the right side of the work area, press Shift+Tab.

The following table describes some of the panels.

Panel	Name	Description
	Swatches	Used to store colors and gradients. It contains different types of swatches, such as color, gradient, and pattern.
	Color	Used to edit and mix colors.
	Stroke	Used to format stroke attributes for shapes and paths.
	Layers	Used to work with layers. This panel lists all the layers in a document starting with the front-most layer. You will learn more about layers later in the course.
	Gradient	Used to apply and adjust gradients.

The Control panel

The Control panel offers a quick alternative to selecting options in panels. By default, the Control panel is docked at the top of the work area. The options in the Control panel vary depending on the type of item you select. For example, if you select a shape or path, the Control panel shows formatting options for the fill and stroke, as well as options for positioning. If you select a text item, the Control panel displays text-formatting options.

The Control panel also provides easy access to some of the basic panels such as the Color, Swatches, Character, and Paragraph panels. This can save time and screen space since you do not have to constantly open and close docked panels based on what you are doing. To view a drop-down panel, click the blue text links. For example, to view the Stroke panel, click the blue Stroke link, as shown in Exhibit 1-7.

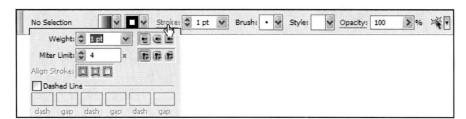

Exhibit 1-7: Example of a drop-down panel via the Control panel

Workspaces

You can perform a variety of tasks with Illustrator, each of which requires a specific set of panels. To make it easier to access and arrange the panels for each task, you can choose a new workspace layout, and/or save your own custom panel configurations. To change the workspace configuration, choose Window, Workspace, [Basic], [Panel], or [Type].

To create a custom workspace:

1 Arrange the panels as you want them.

2 Choose Window, Workspace, Save Workspace.

3 Enter the workspace name and click OK.

To rename or delete workspaces, choose Window, Workspace, Manage Workspaces.

Do it!

A-2: Exploring panels

ACE objective 1.1

Here's how	Here's why
1 Press (TAB)	To hide all the currently open panels, including the Tools panel.
Press (TAB) again	To view the panels again.
2 Press (SHIFT) + (TAB)	To hide just the panel dock on the right side.
Press (SHIFT) + (TAB) again	To view the panel dock again.
3 In the panel dock, click	(The Color icon.) To expand the Color panel.

4 In the Color panel tab, click the ⬦ panel icon	
	(The panel icon is located to the left of the tab name.) The panel contracts to show only the color bar.
Click the icon again	To panel contracts more so that only the tabs are visible.
Click the icon again	To restore the panel to show all the options again.
5 In the panel dock, click 🖌	(The Brushes icon.) To expand the Brushes panel. When you expand the Brushes panel, the Color panel automatically collapses.
6 Point to the Brushes tab, as shown	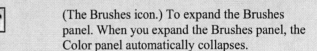
Drag the panel to the left to a blank area of the artboard	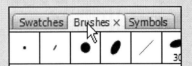
	To undock it from the other panels in the group.
7 Point to the bottom edge of the panel	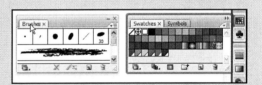
	When the pointer is over the edge of the panel, it changes to show two arrows pointing in opposite directions.
Drag the bottom edge of the panel down	To see more brush patterns.
8 Choose **Window**, **Workspace**, **[Panel]**	The workspace changes—the panels are regrouped based on the default layout, but they are all expanded.
9 Choose **Window**, **Workspace**, **[Basic]**	To return the panels to their original default collapsed locations.

The Tools panel

Explanation

ACE objective 1.1

The Tools panel is docked on the left side of the work area and contains visible and hidden tools you use to select, create, modify, and view artwork and text, as shown in Exhibit 1-8. Similar to the panels on the right side of the work area, you can collapse the Tools panel by clicking the Collapse Dock button. When the Tools panel is collapsed, it shows the tools in a single column. You can also float the Tools panel by dragging the title bar at the top.

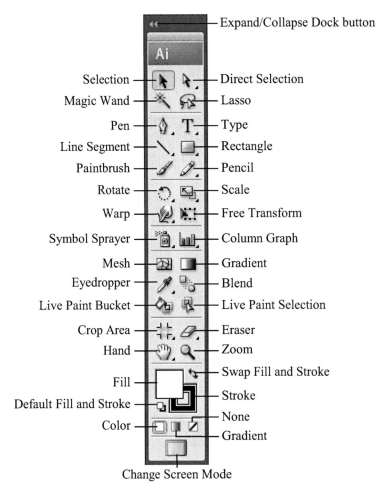

Exhibit 1-8: The Tools panel

The following table describes some of the commonly used tools.

Tool	Description
	The Selection tool is used to select and move items.
	The Direct Selection tool is used to select specific parts of a path.
	The Pen tool is used to create simple and complex paths.
	The Type tool is used to type and modify text.
	The Line Segment tool is used to create simple paths such as straight lines.
	The Rectangle tool is used to create basic shapes.
	The Pencil tool is used to draw freehand paths.
	The Eyedropper tool is used to apply and modify effects, such as color, gradient, and transparency, on items.
	The Crop Area tool is used to crop areas of artwork.
	The Eraser tool is used to erase portions of artwork.
	The Hand tool is used to scroll the artboard.
	The Zoom tool is used to magnify and reduce the display of any area of the artwork.
	The Change Screen Mode button toggles between Maximized Screen Mode, Standard Screen Mode, Full Screen Mode with Menu Bar, and Full Screen Mode.

Tool tips

To identify a tool, button, or a panel option, point to the item for a few seconds. When you do, a tool tip appears that indicates the name and keyboard shortcut.

Hidden tools

Some tools have a small black triangle in the lower-right corner. This indicates there are additional hidden tools. To view and select hidden tools, hold down the mouse button on the visible tool; then point to the tool you want to select and release the mouse button, as shown in Exhibit 1-9. You can also tear off hidden tools into a separate panel. To do this, point to the arrow on the right side of the flyout menu and release the mouse button.

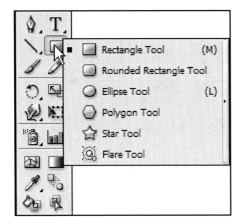

Exhibit 1-9: An example of hidden tools

Do it!

A-3: Exploring the Tools panel

ACE objective 1.1

Here's how	Here's why
1 In the Tools panel, point to ▢	(The Rectangle tool.) A tool tip appears.
2 Press and hold the mouse button on the Rectangle tool	A flyout menu appears, showing hidden shape tools.
Release the mouse button	To close the flyout menu.
3 At the bottom of the Tools panel, click ▭	(The Change Screen Mode button.) A drop-down list appears.
4 From the list, select **Full Screen Mode with Menu Bar**	The work area expands slightly, and the status bar at the bottom is no longer visible.
5 Expand the Change Screen Mode list and select **Maximized Screen Mode**	To switch back to the default view.

Browsing files with Adobe Bridge

Explanation

ACE objective 6.1

Adobe Bridge, shown in Exhibit 1-10, is a helper application that can display a folder full of files as thumbnails or previews, help you organize the files, and open them in the appropriate Adobe Creative Suite application. When bundled with the Creative Suite, it can help you manage projects created with multiple applications, although it also comes with the standalone version of Illustrator. You might want to use Bridge instead of Illustrator's Open dialog box for browsing and opening images.

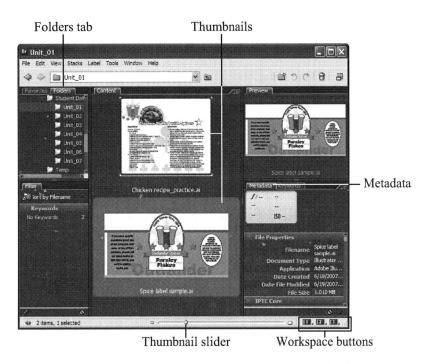

Exhibit 1-10: Adobe Bridge displaying documents in a folder

To manage files with Adobe Bridge:

1 Click the Go to Bridge button in the Control panel.

2 Activate the Folders tab.

3 Navigate to the folder you want by using the tree view.

4 To change the workspace layout, click a workspace button in the lower-right corner.

5 If you want to enlarge or shrink the thumbnails, drag the thumbnail slider.

6 Click a thumbnail to view a preview and metadata (additional information about the file, such as its kind, modification date, and file size).

7 To open a file, double-click its thumbnail to open it in the default Adobe Suite application for that file type, or right-click and select an application from the Open with submenu.

Workspace views

The Bridge window has three workspace buttons in the lower-right corner, as shown in the example in Exhibit 1-10. You can change the workspace view by clicking the buttons, or you can select from other layouts by holding one of the buttons to open a pop-up list, as shown in Exhibit 1-11. You can also use one of the keyboard shortcuts.

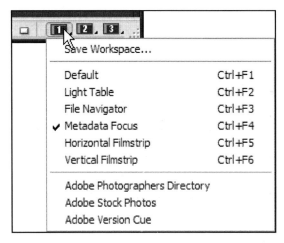

Exhibit 1-11: Changing the Bridge window workspace layout

Do it!

ACE objective 6.1

A-4:   **Managing files with Adobe Bridge**

Here's how	Here's why
1 In the Control panel, click	(The Go to Bridge button.) To start Adobe Bridge. You'll examine the documents in the current unit folders.
2 Activate the Folders tab	(If necessary.) Located in the left pane.
3 In the tree view, navigate to the current unit folder	To display thumbnails for the files within.
4 Observe the workspace buttons at the bottom right corner of the window	There are three buttons: Default, Horizontal Filmstrip, Metadata Focus.
Experiment with the workspace buttons	Click each button and notice what the view looks like.
5 Click	(If necessary.) To return to the default workspace.
6 Drag the thumbnail size slider to the right to enlarge the thumbnails	
7 Click **Chicken recipe_practice**	To display its preview and metadata.
8 Expand the right pane	To view the Metadata information more clearly.
9 Double-click **Chicken recipe_practice**	To open it in Illustrator.
10 Choose **File, Close**	To close the document.
11 Close Adobe Bridge	Activate the window and click the Close button in the top-right corner of the window.

Topic B: Navigation

Explanation

There are several ways to navigate the artboard. You can navigate and view files by using commands in the View menu, the navigation tools, or the Navigator panel.

The View menu

Use the View menu to view and zoom in and out of your illustrations. You can use four commands: Preview, Outline, Overprint Preview, and Pixel Preview. To change the current view, choose a new view from the View menu or use the assigned keyboard shortcuts. The following table describes the views.

View	Shortcut	Description
Preview	Ctrl+Y	Displays the complete illustration as it would appear in print. This is the default view. Using the shortcut Ctrl+Y switches between Preview and Outline view.
Outline	Ctrl+Y	Displays the illustration as it would appear if only the outlines of the artwork were drawn. All paint attributes are hidden in this view, and all items, including overlapping items, are visible, so that you can edit them easily.
Overprint Preview	Alt+Shift+Ctrl+Y	Displays the illustration as it would appear if printed with different colored inks. The color of overlapping areas changes to the color that would result when inks of those colors mix. This view displays only the items for which the Overprint Fill option in the Attributes panel is selected.
Pixel Preview	Alt+Ctrl+Y	Displays the illustration as it would appear if it were a raster image.

The View menu also provides several commands for zooming in and out of your documents. The following table describes the commands.

Command	Shortcut	Description
Zoom in	Ctrl+ +	Increase the magnification by a preset percentage. To use the shortcut for this command, you must press the + key at the top of the keyboard.
Zoom out	Ctrl+ -	Reduce the magnification by a preset percentage.
Fit in Window	Ctrl+0	Automatically fits the artboard to the size of the application window. This might set the magnification of the illustration above or below 100% depending on the size of the artboard.
Actual Size	Ctrl+1	Shows the illustration at 100% magnification.

Do it!   **B-1:   Using Views**

Here's how	Here's why
1 Observe the large ellipse in the middle of the label	
	Notice that the bottom of the ellipse is not completely visible.
2 Choose **View**, **Outline**	(Or press Ctrl+Y.) To view the outlines of the illustration. The complete outline of the ellipse is now visible. Earlier, you could see only a part of the ellipse because the remaining part was hidden behind the gold and white rectangles.
Choose **View**, **Preview**	To switch back to the Preview view.
3 Press ⊂CTRL⊃ + ⊂+⊃ three times	(Or choose View, Zoom In.) To take a closer look at the illustration.
Observe the Zoom box	It shows the current magnification.
4 Press ⊂CTRL⊃ + ⊂0⊃	(Or choose View, Fit in Window.) To see the entire artboard again.

Remind students to press the + key at the top of the keyboard, not the + key to the right of the number pad.

Navigation tools

Explanation You can navigate a document by using either the Zoom tool or the Hand tool. The Hand tool is used to reposition the artboard to view different areas of an illustration, which is useful when you are viewing an illustration at a higher magnification. To use the Hand tool, select it in the Tools panel, then drag anywhere on the artboard to scroll it so that a different area is visible.

You can also temporarily access the Hand tool without having to select it in the Tools panel by pressing the Spacebar. When you are done using the Hand tool, release the Spacebar to return to the previous tool.

You can use the Zoom tool to magnify specific areas of an illustration. When you select the Zoom tool from the Tools panel, the pointer changes to the shape of a magnifying glass with a plus sign in its center. You then click on an area that you want to view at a higher magnification. The point you click will be centered and the image magnified. You can also zoom in on a specific area by dragging the Zoom tool diagonally across the area. When you release the mouse button, the rectangle you made will be magnified to fill the screen.

To zoom out, select the Zoom tool and press Alt and click. When you press Alt, the pointer changes to the shape of a magnifying glass with a minus sign in its center.

You can also zoom in and out by holding down the Alt key and rolling the mouse wheel.

The Navigator panel

The Navigator panel displays the artwork as a thumbnail. You can use this panel to change magnification, zoom in on a specific area of the illustration, or drag the view of the artboard so that a specific area is visible.

To display the Navigator panel, shown in Exhibit 1-12, choose Window, Navigator. The panel displays a thumbnail of the artwork on a white background. If the illustration is magnified, the visible portions in the work area are defined within a red square, called the Proxy Preview Area. You can change the view of the illustration in the work area by moving the box on the thumbnail. The panel also provides a zoom slider you can drag to zoom in and out. You can click the Zoom In and Zoom Out buttons to change the magnification, and the Zoom box displays the current magnification. You can enter a number in this box to quickly zoom to a specific magnification value.

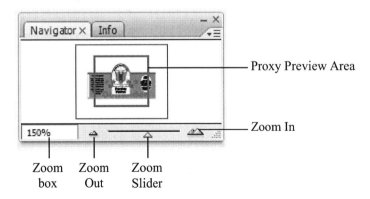

Exhibit 1-12: The Navigator panel

Do it!   **B-2:   Using the Navigation tools**

Here's how	Here's why
1 In the Tools panel, click [🔍]	(The Zoom tool.) You can also press Z. Notice that the pointer changes to the shape of a magnifying glass with a plus sign in the center.
2 Click the text in the white ellipse on the right side of the label	The magnification in the Zoom box changes and the text is centered and magnified.
Magnify the text to 400%	(By clicking the text several times.) Now the text fills the viewing area.
3 Press and hold (SPACEBAR)	So that the pointer temporarily changes to a hand icon.
While pressing (SPACEBAR), drag the artboard to the right	(If necessary.) So that the center of the label is visible.
4 Release (SPACEBAR) and press and hold (ALT)	Notice that when Alt is pressed, the pointer changes to a magnifying glass with a minus sign in its center.
Click anywhere in the artboard	To zoom out. The area you clicked is now centered in the artboard.
5 In the Tools panel, double-click the Zoom tool	To switch to the actual size of the illustration.
6 In the Tools panel, double-click the Hand tool	To switch to the Fit in Window view. Now the entire artboard is visible.

Topic C: Adobe Help Viewer

Explanation

Adobe provides an exhaustive, easily navigable Help system to obtain information about features, tools, and commands for all of the applications in the Creative Suite series. You can use the Adobe Help Viewer to search for topics specifically related to Illustrator.

Adobe Help Viewer

To open the Help Viewer, choose Help, Illustrator Help, or press F1. When you do, Adobe Help Viewer appears, and Illustrator CS3 is selected automatically in the Browse box, as shown in Exhibit 1-13. The Help Viewer is divided into two panes: a navigation pane on the left and a topic pane on the right. The navigation pane contains links to various topics. You can click a topic link and view its related content in the topic pane. The home page in the topic pane contains four links you can use to access additional resources and information about new features in Illustrator CS3.

You can search for information strictly within Illustrator help files, or within any other Adobe applications installed on your computer. If you know specifically what you want help with, you can enter keywords in the Search box at the top of the window and press Enter. The Help Viewer searches the help files for instances of the keywords, and a new list of links is presented.

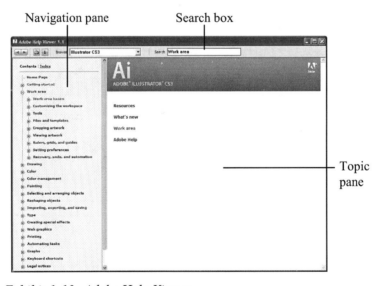

Exhibit 1-13: Adobe Help Viewer

Do it!

C-1:   Using Help

Here's how	Here's why
1 Choose **Help, Illustrator Help...**	(Or press F1.)
2 Expand the Browse list	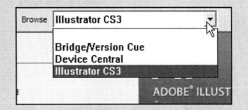

	(Click the small triangle on the right side of the Browse box.) You can search for information only within Illustrator help files, or within other Adobe applications installed on your computer. (If you have other applications installed on your computer, they'll be visible in list.)
Press ESC	To close the list.
3 In the Topic pane, click **What's new**	The Topic pane changes to show several links explaining what's new in Illustrator CS3.
Click **Advanced drawing tools and controls**	The Topic pane changes again to provide some basic information about changes to some of the tools.
	The Navigation pane shows a basic list of help categories.
4 In the Navigation pane, click **Work area**	The Topic pane changes to show links related to the work area. You can also expand the list as a hierarchy within the Navigation pane.
5 In the Navigation pane, click the small plus sign (+) to the left of Work area	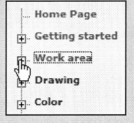
	To expand it. The Navigation pane now shows the same links as the Topic pane.
6 In the Navigation pane, expand **Work area basics**	Click the small plus sign to the left of the link.
Click **Workspace overview**	To show workspace information in the Topic pane.
	You can also search Help by using keywords.

7 At the top of the Help Viewer, in the Search box, enter **draw a circle**	
Press (↵ ENTER)	A list of links that contain the specified keywords appears. Adobe searches the help files for all applications but shows the results for Illustrator CS3, since that is the application you specified.
8 Click **Draw ellipses**	The Topic pane displays the steps to draw an ellipse.
9 Close Adobe Help Viewer	(Click the "x" in the top-right corner of the window.) To return to Illustrator.
10 Close the document without saving changes	When prompted to save, click No.

Unit summary: Getting started

Topic A   In this topic, you learned how to start Illustrator, and you explored **the Illustrator environment**.

Topic B   In this topic, you learned how to **navigate an Illustrator document**.

Topic C   In this topic, you used **Adobe Help Viewer** to search for help in using Illustrator.

Independent practice activity

In this activity, you'll open an existing Illustrator document and navigate around it. You'll show/hide panels, zoom in on certain portions of the artwork, switch viewing modes, and use the Hand tool. You'll also open Adobe Help Viewer to find information about how to draw a rectangle.

1 Open the Chicken recipe_practice document (in the current unit folder).

2 View the artwork without the Tools panel and the panels. (*Hint*: Press Tab.)

3 Show the Tools panel and panels again.

4 View the artwork in Outline view. (*Hint*: Choose View, Outline, or press Ctrl+Y.)

5 Switch back to Preview view.

6 Zoom in on the spice shakers in the upper-left corner of the recipe. Zoom in to 300%. (*Hint*: Use the Zoom tool.)

7 Using the Hand tool, drag to the right so that the image of the plate of chicken is visible. (*Hint*: Press Spacebar to temporarily access the Hand tool.)

8 Zoom out to 50%. (*Hint*: Use the Zoom box.)

9 Fit the entire artboard in the work area. (*Hint*: Choose View, Fit in Window, or press Ctrl+0.)

10 Open Adobe Help Viewer. (*Hint*: Choose Help, Illustrator Help, or press F1.)

11 Using Adobe Help Viewer, find information about how to draw a rectangle. (*Hint*: In the Search box enter "draw a rectangle," and press Enter.)

12 Close Adobe Help Viewer.

13 Close the document without saving any changes.

Review questions

1 Which type of graphic can you enlarge significantly without it appearing jagged when printed?

   A Raster

   B Vector

   C Bitmap

   D JPEG

2 Which panel is not available in the Illustrator work area by default?

   A Control panel

   B Tools panel

   C Color panel

   D Pathfinder panel

3 Which panel can you use to create custom fill and stroke colors?

   A Control panel

   B Swatches panel

   C Color panel

   D Tools panel

4 Which panel provides quick access to options related to selected items?

   A Swatches panel

   B Color panel

   C Tools panel

   D Control panel

5 Which statements about the Control panel are true? (Choose all that apply.)

   A The options in the Control panel change depending on what is selected in an illustration.

   B The Control panel shows options for working with shapes and paths only.

   C You can access drop-down panels by clicking on the blue links in the Control panel.

   D The Control panel is locked at the top of the work area.

6 How can you show any hidden options in a panel? (Choose all that apply.)

   A From the panel menu, choose Show Options.

   B Click the small panel icon on the left side of the panel tab.

   C No panels in Illustrator have hidden options.

   D Double-click the panel tab.

7 How can you save an arrangement of panels so you can return to it later?

   A Choose Illustrator, Preferences, General, Workspaces.

   B Choose Window, Workspace, Save Workspace.

   C Choose Illustrator, Preferences, Save Workspace.

   D Choose Window, Workspace, [Minimal].

8 How can you zoom in on a selected object? (Choose all that apply.)

   A Choose a magnification from the Zoom list.

   B In the Tools panel, select the Hand tool, and then click or drag across the selected item.

   C Choose View, Zoom In.

   D In the Tools panel, select the Zoom tool, and then click or drag across the selected item.

9 Which view displays an object's paths without any paint attributes?

   A Preview

   B Outline

   C Overprint Preview

   D Pixel Preview

10 Pressing the Spacebar and dragging on the artboard performs which action?

   A Accesses the Zoom tool temporarily and creates a zoom marquee.

   B Accesses the Selection tool temporarily and drags the selected item.

   C Accesses the Hand tool temporarily and drags the document to scroll it.

   D Accesses the Zoom Out tool temporarily and zooms out.

11 Which are tasks can you accomplish using Adobe Bridge? (Choose all that apply.)

   A Display folders of files as thumbnails or previews.

   B Open files in their appropriate Adobe Creative Suite applications.

   C Transfer text and graphics into files created in other Adobe Creative Suite applications.

   D Organize files.

12 How can you open Adobe Bridge from within Illustrator?

   A Choose File, Go to Bridge.

   B Right-click on a blank area of the artboard, and then choose Go to Bridge from the pop-up menu.

   C Click the Go to Bridge button in the Control panel.

   D Double-click on a blank area of the artboard.

13 Which are ways you can browse topics in the Help Viewer? (Choose all that apply.)

   A Click a link in the Navigation pane.

   B In the Search box, type a term you want to search for, then press Enter.

   C Select the Topic pane, and then begin typing what you are looking for to automatically jump to that topic.

   D Activate the Index link in the Navigation pane, then click the letter under which you want to search.

Unit 2

Creating a simple illustration

Unit time: 65 minutes

Complete this unit, and you'll know how to:

A Create and save a new document.

B Create basic shapes by using the shape tools, and draw shapes precisely by using keyboard shortcuts.

C Select shapes by using several techniques, and scale, duplicate, align and distribute, merge, group, rotate, and adjust the stacking order of shapes.

D Export an illustration.

Topic A: Create a new document

This topic covers the following ACE exam objectives for Illustrator CS3.

#	Objective
1.3	Given a scenario, select and configure the appropriate settings in the Document Setup dialog box.
1.4	Given a scenario, select the appropriate New Document preset. (Scenarios include: Print, web, and mobile documents.)
7.3	Prepare a document for printing by choosing and configuring the appropriate resolution and rasterization settings.
8.2	List and describe the options available for saving Illustrator documents by using the Illustrator Legacy Options dialog box.

New document settings

Explanation

To begin creating an illustration, you need to first set up a new document. In Illustrator, you can choose settings for your documents based on how you want to output the illustration once you are finished with it. Some of these options include deciding on the color mode you want and the width and height of the artboard. You can set the options you want individually, or use a document profile preset with some basic options.

Creating a new document

ACE objective 1.4

To create a new document:

1 Choose File, New to open the New Document dialog box.

2 In the Name box, enter a descriptive name for the document.

3 From the New Document Profile list, select a profile preset based on how you want to use the document. For example, if your end goal is to use the artwork on a Web page, you can select the Web profile to automatically establish basic settings favorable for that type of output.

4 If necessary, from the Size list, select the artboard size you want. You can also set a custom size by entering values in the Width and Height boxes.

5 If necessary, from the Units list, select the unit of measure you want.

6 To the left of Advanced, click the arrows to expand the dialog box, as shown in Exhibit 2-1.

7 If necessary, from the Color Mode list, select either CMYK or RGB. Generally, CMYK color is used for illustrations you plan to print on a four-color printer. RGB illustrations are commonly used for illustrations you plan to incorporate into Web pages or perhaps print to an office printer that uses the RGB color model.

8 If necessary, specify a resolution for raster effects. This is covered more fully later in the course.

9 If necessary, select a different preview mode for the document.

10 Click OK to create the new document.

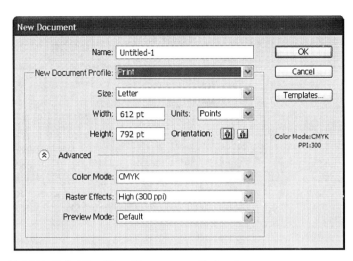

Exhibit 2-1: The New Document dialog box

Saving a document

To save a document:

1   Choose File, Save As to open the Save As dialog box.
2   From the Save in list, select the folder where you want to save the file.
3   In the File name box, specify the name of the file, if necessary. The default extension for files created in Illustrator CS3 is .ai.
4   Click Save. The Illustrator Options dialog box appears, as shown in Exhibit 2-2.
5   Set the options you want for the Illustrator file and click OK.

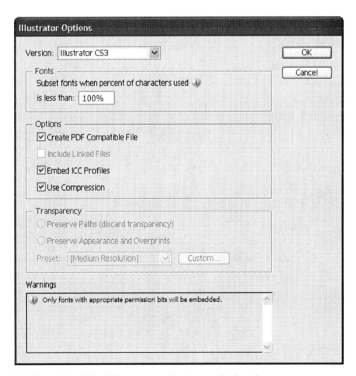

Exhibit 2-2: The Illustrator Options dialog box

The following table describes some of the options available in the Illustrator Options dialog box.

ACE objective 8.2

Option	Description
Fonts	If an illustration uses text, you might want to embed the fonts used in the document. That way, if the document is opened on a computer without the fonts, it will still display as intended. The subset fonts box specifies when to embed the entire font (as opposed to just the characters used in the document) based on how many of the font's characters are used. For instance, if a font contains 1,000 characters, but the document uses only 10 of those characters, you might decide that embedding the font is not worth the extra file size. By default, the box is set to 100%, indicating that if the text does not use all the characters in the fonts used in the illustration, they will not be embedded.
Create PDF Compatible File	Saves a PDF representation of the document in the Illustrator file. This option makes the Illustrator file compatible with other Adobe applications, and applications that can import PDF files, although it does increase the file size.
Include Linked Files	Embeds linked artwork in the file.
Embed ICC Profiles	Creates a color-managed document so that colors appear the same from device to device.
Use Compression	Compresses PDF data. Using compression increases the time required to save the file, but decreases file size.

Backsaving documents

You might want to backsave a CS3 document to a prior version of Illustrator so that you can open it on another computer. You can open native CS3 documents using a prior version of Illustrator, but if your artwork is complex and uses features only available in CS3, Illustrator will need to convert some of the content in a way that the prior version of Illustrator can render. Older versions will have more trouble rendering certain types of content than newer versions. To help avoid the amount of changes, you can backsave CS3 documents to earlier versions of Illustrator. To do so, select the version of Illustrator you want to backsave the document to from the Version list in the Illustrator Options dialog box, shown in Exhibit 2-2.

Do it!

A-1:   Creating a new document

Here's how	Here's why
1 Choose **File**, **New...**	To open the New Document dialog box.
2 In the Name box, enter **Spice shaker illustration**	

Students can also press Ctrl+N to open the dialog box.

3 Expand the New Document Profile list

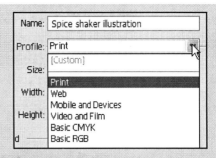

The list shows presets for different types of content.

4 Verify that **Print** is selected, then close the list

By default, the Print preset sets the unit of measurement as points. You'll change the unit of measurement to inches.

5 From the Units list, select **Inches**

6 In the Width box, enter **8**

In the Height box, enter **10**

To create a custom-sized artboard.

7 Click

The Landscape orientation button.

8 To the left of Advanced, click ⏬

To expand the dialog box.

9 In the Color Mode list, verify that **CMYK** is selected

10 Click **OK**

A new blank artboard appears. You'll save the document.

11 Choose **File**, **Save As...**

To open the Save As dialog box.

Navigate to the current unit folder

(If necessary.) The file is already named "Spice shaker illustration" based on what you entered in the New Document dialog box. You'll leave the file name as it is.

12 Click **Save**

To open the Illustrator Options dialog box. You'll leave the current default settings as they are.

13 Click **OK**

To save the file.

Document Setup

After creating a document, you might need to change some of its properties, such as the artboard size, controls for typography, and how it displays and exports transparent objects. You can adjust these settings by choosing File, Document Setup, and selecting a category from the list at the top. The Artboard settings, shown in Exhibit 2-3, include settings for artboard size and for viewing artwork as outlines instead of displaying detail.

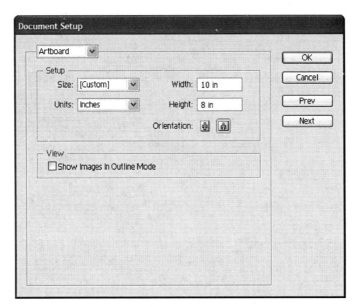

Exhibit 2-3: The Artboard settings in the Document Setup dialog box

In the Type settings, shown in Exhibit 2-4, you can choose to highlight type problems, to automatically convert straight quotation marks to curved typographical ones as you type, and to control the size of superscripted, subscripted, or small caps text. You can also choose whether or not text should remain editable in exported files (at the possible expense of a different appearance if the new user doesn't have the exact fonts you used).

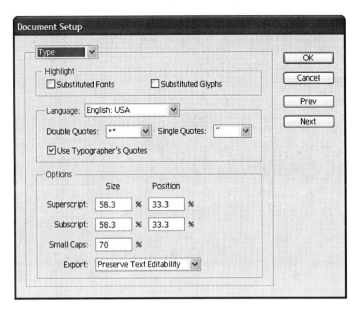

Exhibit 2-4: The Type settings in the Document Setup dialog box

You can use the Transparency settings, shown in Exhibit 2-5, to control how the Transparency Grid displays areas that are opaque and transparent. (To view the Transparency Grid, choose View, Show Transparency Grid.) Additionally, you can choose how Illustrator converts transparent objects to solid ones when exporting because other applications don't usually handle transparency directly.

ACE objective 7.3

For example, if a red semi-transparent shape overlaps a yellow shape, the intersection yields a third color (orange). Illustrator could either render that area as another vector object or convert all of the objects to raster (which is usually necessary only for complex illustrations with many overlaps of multi-colored objects). You can use the presets and custom settings in the Document Setup dialog box to choose the resolution of raster objects Illustrator exports, and to specify how complex the illustration must be to export raster images to simulate the transparency in the original image.

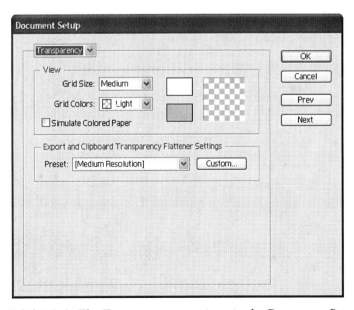

Exhibit 2-5: The Transparency settings in the Document Setup dialog box

Do it!

A-2: Changing document setup

ACE objective 1.3

Here's how	Here's why
1 Choose **File**, **Document Setup...**	You've decided that the artboard should be the size of letter paper.
2 From the category list, select **Artboard**	If necessary.
3 From the Size list, select **Letter**	To set the artboard to 11 x 8.5 inches.
4 Click **OK**	
5 Choose **File**, **Save**	(Or press Ctrl+S.) To update the document.

Remind students that they can also press Ctrl+S to update the document.

Topic B: Basic shapes

This topic covers the following ACE exam objectives for Illustrator CS3.

#	Objective
1.2	Explain how to use grids, guides, and rulers.
2.1	Given a tool, create an object. (Tools include: Pen, shape tools, and Pathfinder.)

Explanation

You can create interesting and sometimes complex-looking illustrations by using simple combinations of shapes such as rectangles, squares, or circles.

Creating basic shapes

ACE objective 2.1

You can draw basic shapes, such as rectangles, ellipses, stars, and polygons, using the shape tools in the Tools panel. To do so, select the tool, then drag in the artboard to create that shape. The Ellipse and Rectangle tools create shapes exactly as you drag them. For example, you can create rectangles of all sizes and dimensions. To create proportional shapes, such as squares or circles, press Shift while dragging. The Star and Polygon tools always create proportional shapes. Pressing Shift restricts them from rotating.

B-1: Creating basic shapes

Here's how	Here's why
1 In the Tools panel, click 	(The Rectangle tool.) You'll begin by creating some rectangle and ellipse shapes.
2 Point near the top-left side of the artboard, and drag down and to the right, as shown	 To begin creating a rectangle.
Release the mouse button	To create the rectangle.
3 In the Tools panel, click and hold the Rectangle tool	To see the tool flyout menu.
From the flyout menu, select the Ellipse tool	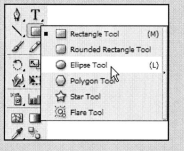
4 In the artboard, to the right of the rectangle, drag down and to the right	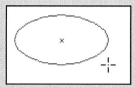 To create an ellipse. You'll also create a circle.
5 Point to a blank area of the artboard	
Press and hold (SHIFT)	Pressing Shift keeps the circle proportional.
Drag down and to the right	Lastly, you'll create a star.
6 From the Ellipse tool flyout, select the Star tool	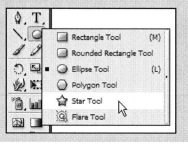

7	In the artboard, drag to begin creating a star	Don't release the mouse button.
	As you drag, press `SHIFT`	To keep the star from rotating.
	Release the mouse button	To create the star.
8	Choose **File**, **Save**	(Or press Ctrl+S.) To update the document.

Remind students they can also press Ctrl+S to update the document.

Drawing shapes precisely

Explanation

For some shape tools, you can modify shapes as you draw. For example, by default shapes are drawn from the point you start to drag, to the point where you stop. To create a shape starting from its center, press Alt and point to the location where you want the center of the shape to be, then drag until the shape attains the required size.

Also, you can modify how some shapes appear as you draw. For example, by default the Star tool creates a star with five points. To increase or decrease the number of points, press the Up or Down arrow keys while dragging. You can also use the same technique to make the corners of a rectangle more rounded.

Specifying precise measurements

You might want to create shapes that have exact dimensions. To do this, select the tool for the shape you want to create, and click the artboard. A dialog box appears in which you can enter the width and height or the radius information that you want, as shown in Exhibit 2-6. After you enter the dimensions you want, click OK. The shape appears where you initially clicked.

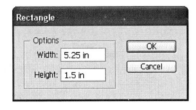
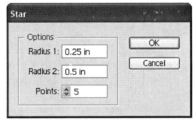

Exhibit 2-6: Examples of dialog boxes for creating shapes with precise measurements

Positioning shapes as you draw

You can position a shape as you draw it. To do this, press the Spacebar while dragging to temporarily have the freedom to reposition the shape on the artboard. Release the Spacebar to continue drawing the shape.

Rulers, guides, and the grid

ACE objective 1.2

You can use rulers, guides, and the grid to resize and position objects precisely. To view the rulers, choose View, Show Rulers (or press Ctrl+R). When you do, rulers appear horizontally at the top of the artboard, and vertically at the left side. The unit of measurement for the rulers depends on what you specified when you created the document. To change the unit of measurement for the rulers, choose File, Document Setup, and choose a different unit of measurement from the Units list.

You can place guides in the work area to help position objects. In order to create guides, the rulers need to be visible. Point to either the horizontal or vertical ruler bar, then drag into the work area to create a guide. You can also manipulate guides in the following ways:

- To reposition or delete guides, drag them in the work area, or select them and press Delete. You can choose View, Guides, Clear Guides to delete all guides at one time.

- To lock guides, choose View, Guides, Lock Guides. When guides are locked, you cannot select or reposition them. However, you can still add new guides to the work area. To unlock guides, choose View, Guides, Lock Guides again to deselect the option.

- To change guide settings, choose Edit, Preferences, Guides & Grid. You can change the guide color (which are cyan by default), or change the guide style from lines to dots.

The grid is a series of vertical and horizontal lines that appear behind your artwork, but do not print and are not visible in your artwork if you export it. To view the grid, choose View, Show Grid (or press Ctrl+"). To change the spacing between gridlines, choose Edit, Preferences, Guides & Grid. Under Grid, you can edit the style, color, and distance between lines.

Do it!

B-2: Drawing shapes precisely

Here's how	Here's why
1 Select the Selection tool, and click the ellipse	To select it. You'll delete the ellipse, circle, and rectangle shapes and create new ones that are specific sizes.
Press `DELETE`	To delete the ellipse.
2 Select and delete the rectangle and circle	

ACE objective 1.2

3 Choose **View**, **Show Rulers**	(Or press Ctrl+R.) To view the rulers.
4 Choose **View**, **Show Grid**	(Or press Ctrl+".) To view the grid.
5 Select the Rectangle tool	Press down on the Star tool and select the Rectangle tool from the flyout menu.
6 Point to the artboard at the intersection of the 1-inch mark on the horizontal ruler and the 8 inch mark on the vertical ruler	
Drag to create a rectangle that is 1 inch wide and 2 inches tall	You can also create shapes with exact dimensions by clicking.
7 Select the Ellipse tool	Press down on the Rectangle tool and select the Ellipse tool from the flyout menu.
8 Click once on a blank part of the artboard	To open the Ellipse dialog box.
In the Width box, enter **1.25**	
In the Height box, enter **.5**	
Click **OK**	To create an ellipse that is 1¼ inches wide and ½ inch tall.
	You'll also create a star that has more than five points.

9 Select the Star tool

Press down on the Ellipse tool and select the Star tool from the flyout menu.

In the artboard, drag to begin creating a star

Without releasing the mouse button, press ⬆ four times

To add four more points to the star.

Press SHIFT, and release the mouse button

To create the star shape.

Lastly, you'll position a circle on the star to create a sun.

10 Select the Ellipse tool

Demonstrate the next few steps for students if necessary.

Press and hold SHIFT + ALT, and drag in the artboard to begin creating a circle from the center out

11 Without releasing SHIFT + ALT and the mouse button, press SPACEBAR

To temporarily move the shape to a new location.

Remind students as they draw the circle not to release the mouse button until the circle is exactly as they want it.

Center the circle on the star, then release SPACEBAR to continue sizing the circle

12 Resize and position the circle as shown and release the mouse button

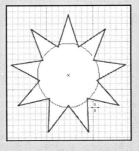

To create the sun.

13 Select the Selection tool and click a blank area of the artboard

To deselect the circle and view the results.

14 Update the document

Press Ctrl+S.

Topic C: Manipulate shapes

This topic covers the following ACE exam objectives for Illustrator CS3.

#	Objective
2.2	Given a scenario, choose the appropriate tool to select an object or the points of an object. (Scenarios or tools include: Selection tool, Direct Selection tool, Isolation mode, Select menu commands.)
2.3	Given a scenario, transform objects. (Scenarios include: Rotate, reflect, and scale an object; Transform Again; Align (Align to Artboard, Align to Crop, Align and Distribute Points).)
2.15	Create and modify compound shapes by using Pathfinder panel or the Eraser tool.

Transforming and aligning shapes

Explanation

As you work with Illustrator more, you will need to manipulate existing shapes. This could include scaling, moving, rotating, or aligning and distributing them. In Illustrator, you can manipulate shapes individually, or you can manipulate multiple shapes simultaneously.

Selecting shapes

ACE objective 2.2

You can use the following techniques to select shapes:

- By using the Selection tool, click a shape to select it.
- To select multiple shapes, click a shape to select it, then press Shift and click the additional shapes you want to select.
- Use the Selection tool to create a marquee by dragging around all or part of the shape(s) you want to select.
- Use the Lasso tool to drag around all or part of the shape(s) you want to select.

Bounding boxes

When you select one or more shapes, a bounding box appears around the shape(s), as shown in Exhibit 2-7. You can use the bounding box to move, rotate, duplicate, and scale shapes easily by manipulating the bounding box handles (the hollow squares along the border of the bounding box).

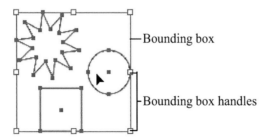

Exhibit 2-7: An example of a bounding box

Scaling shapes

ACE objective 2.3

Scaling a shape refers to enlarging or reducing it. You can scale shapes horizontally, vertically, or both. The following table describes methods for scaling shapes.

Method	Description
Selection tool	Click a shape to make its bounding box visible. Point to a handle on the bounding box until the pointer changes to a double-headed arrow, then drag to scale the shape larger or smaller. To scale a shape proportionally, press Shift as you drag. To scale a shape proportionally from the center out, press Shift+Alt as you drag.
Scale tool	With a shape selected, using the Scale tool, drag any direction to scale the shape from the center out. To scale a shape proportionally, press Shift as you drag.
Control panel	Select a shape, in the Control panel click the Transform link to view the Transform drop-down panel, shown in Exhibit 2-8. In the W and H boxes, enter values to set the width and height you want for the shape. To scale a shape proportionally, click the Lock Proportions icon to the right of the W and H boxes, enter a value in one of the boxes, and the other box will adjust automatically.

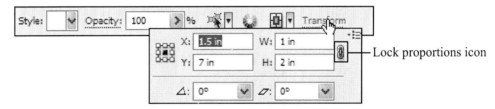

Exhibit 2-8: The Transform drop-down panel in the Control panel

Reference points

When you scale a shape by using the Scale tool or the Control panel, the shape becomes bigger or smaller based on a reference point. By default, the reference point is the center of the shape, but you can change the reference point to adjust the way the shape behaves as you resize it.

To change the reference point using the Scale tool, click once anywhere in the artboard to create a new reference point, then move the pointer away from the reference point and drag to scale the shape.

To change the reference point by using the Control panel, expand the Transform drop-down panel, then click a new reference point on the reference point locator (shown in Exhibit 2-9), and enter values in the Width and Height boxes as necessary.

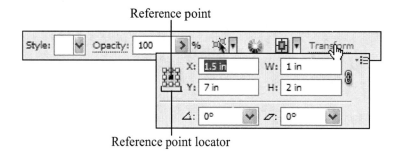

Exhibit 2-9: The Reference point locater in the Transform panel

C-1:   Selecting and scaling shapes

Here's how	Here's why

1 Press `CTRL` + `–` two or three times

To zoom out. You'll move some of the shapes to the scratch area to free up space on the artboard.

2 Press `SHIFT`, then click the ellipse and the rectangle

To select both shapes.

Drag the shapes from the artboard to the scratch area

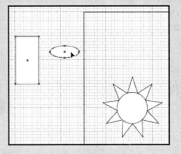

3 Press `CTRL` + `0`

To fit the artboard in the application window. First, you'll resize the star so that it is 1 inch tall and wide.

4 Select the five-point star

Select the Selection tool if necessary, and click the star.

5 In the Control panel, click the blue Transform link

To view the Transform drop-down panel.

6 In the W and H boxes, change the value to **1**

To change the size of the star to 1 inch.

Click a blank area of the artboard

To collapse the panel.

7 Position the star in the lower-left corner of the artboard

You'll also make the sun much larger.

8 Using the Selection tool, point to the empty space next to the sun shape, as shown

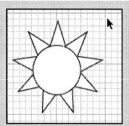

Drag across the sun shape

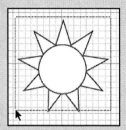

(To select both the star and the circle.) As you do this, you don't have to drag across the entire shape to include it in the selection. Only part of the shape needs to be included in the selection box.

9 Point to the upper-right bounding box handle

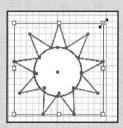

The pointer changes to show two arrows pointing in opposite directions.

Slowly drag up and to the right

The shapes are larger, but are no longer exactly proportional. You'll resize the sun so that it stays proportional.

10 Press `CTRL` + `Z`

To undo the change.

11 Press and hold `SHIFT`, then drag the upper-right handle up and to the right

Resize the sun so that it is approximately 6 inches wide

It doesn't have to be exact. (You might want to reposition the sun on the artboard to resize it more easily.)

12 Reposition the large sun near the left side of the artboard

13 Choose **View**, **Hide Grid**

(Or press Ctrl+".) To hide the artboard grid.

14 Update the document

Press Ctrl+S.

Duplicate shapes

Explanation

There are two ways to duplicate shapes in Illustrator. One way is to select a shape, and then choose Edit, Copy (Ctrl+C), and then Edit, Paste (Ctrl+V). This method places the duplicate in the center of the visible artboard.

You can also duplicate a shape by pressing Alt and dragging the selected shape. When you do, the pointer changes to two pointers, one overlapping the other, as shown in Exhibit 2-10. This is a visual indication that you are duplicating the shape. You can maintain the alignment of the duplicate shape to the original shape by pressing Alt+Shift as you drag.

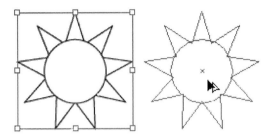

Exhibit 2-10: An example of duplicating a shape by pressing Alt and dragging

C-2:   Duplicating shapes

Here's how	Here's why
1 Select the small five-point star	(Near the bottom-left corner of the artboard.) You'll create duplicates of the star that will run along the bottom of the artboard.
2 Press (ALT), and drag the star to the right	To create a duplicate of the star.
3 Create three more duplicates of the star across the bottom of the artboard	(Press Alt and drag one of the stars to the right.) You'll also create a duplicate of the ellipse to begin creating a spice shaker.
4 Press (CTRL) + (-) twice	To zoom out so that the shapes in the scratch area are visible.
5 From the scratch area, move the ellipse to the right side of the artboard	
Press (CTRL) + (0)	To fit the artboard in the application window. You want to create a duplicate ellipse and keep it vertically aligned with the original ellipse.
6 Press (ALT), and drag the ellipse down	To create a duplicate ellipse.
As you drag, press (SHIFT)	Pressing Shift keeps the duplicate from shifting to the left or right.
Position the duplicate ellipse as shown, and release the mouse button	
7 Update the document	

Let students know it doesn't matter if they are aligned or spaced evenly.

Align and distribute shapes

Explanation

ACE objective 2.3

It can be tedious to manually line up multiple shapes, or to make sure they are spaced evenly. You can use the Align panel (shown in Exhibit 2-11) to precisely and easily arrange shapes. To align shapes, select the shapes you want to align, and click an alignment button under Align Objects in the Align panel. Similarly, to distribute shapes, click a distribution button under Distribute Objects. You can also access the alignment and distribute buttons in the Control panel when multiple objects are selected.

When you distribute shapes, the outside shapes remain fixed, and the inside shapes shift so that they are evenly distributed. For example, suppose you have four rectangles that you want to distribute evenly horizontally. With the rectangles selected, clicking one of the Horizontal Distribute buttons forces the middle rectangles to be evenly distributed between the right-most and left-most rectangles.

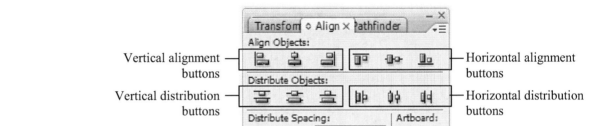

Vertical alignment buttons — Horizontal alignment buttons
Vertical distribution buttons — Horizontal distribution buttons

Exhibit 2-11: The Align panel

Distribute spacing

By default, the distribution buttons distribute shapes evenly between the outer two shapes (either horizontally or vertically). You can also distribute shapes by using exact distances between their paths.

To distribute shapes by using exact distances between them:

1   Select the shapes to distribute.
2   If necessary, choose Show Options from the panel menu to see the distribute spacing options (shown in Exhibit 2-11).
3   In the Distribute Spacing box, enter the amount of space that should appear between shapes.
4   Using the Selection tool, click the shape from which you want the other shapes to distribute. The shape you click will remain fixed in its position.
5   Click either the Vertical Distribute Space button or the Horizontal Distribute Space button.

C-3: Aligning and distributing shapes

Here's how	Here's why
1 Select all the stars at the bottom of the artboard	(Point to a blank area to the left of the first star, then drag across all of them to select them.) You'll vertically align the stars, and distribute them.
2 In the Control panel, click the blue Align link	To view the Align drop-down panel.
3 Under Align Objects, click	(The Vertical Align Center button.) The stars shift so that they are vertically aligned. You'll also distribute the stars so that there is ¼ inch of space between them.
4 Click on the left-most star	To select it as the starting item.
5 Expand the Align panel again	Click the blue Align link in the Control panel.
6 In the Distribute Spacing box, change the value to **.25**	
Under Distribute Spacing, click	(The Horizontal Distribute Space button.) To distribute the stars horizontally ¼ inch apart.
7 Deselect the stars	To view the results.
8 Update the document	

Using Shape Mode commands

Explanation

ACE objective 2.15

You can merge, divide, and combine shapes by using the Shape Mode commands in the Pathfinder panel, shown in Exhibit 2-12. This is often an efficient way to create complex shapes.

Exhibit 2-12: The Shape Mode commands in the Pathfinder panel

There are four shape mode commands, all of which are briefly explained in the following table. The most powerful command is the Add to Shape Area button, which will be the main focus of this section. The Add to Shape Area command creates complex shapes (called compound shapes) based on groups of simple shapes.

Button	Shape Mode	Description
	Add To Shape Area	Traces the outline of shapes so that they appear as a single shape. The shape you end up with uses the fill and stroke attributes of the top shape in the stacking order. You can still manipulate the individual shapes.
	Subtract From Shape Area	Subtracts the front-most shapes from the back-most shape.
	Intersect Shape Areas	Traces the outline of the area overlapped by all the shapes.
	Exclude Overlapping Shape Areas	Traces the non-overlapping areas of the shapes. The overlapping areas will then become transparent. Areas in which an even number of shapes overlap are transparent, and areas in which an odd number of shapes overlap are filled.

Compound shapes

When you use the Add to Shape Area command, the selected shapes are combined into a *compound shape*. A compound shape is a shape in which two or more shapes are partially combined to act as one shape, but can still be individually manipulated. In Exhibit 2-13, the first example (on the left) shows several overlapping shapes. The second example shows the results of using the Add to Shape Area command, which combined the shapes into one compound shape. Even though the objects appear as one shape, you can still manipulate the individual components by using the Direct Selection tool, as shown in the third example. Once you select an individual component of a compound shape, you can manipulate it to change the overall compound shape, as shown in the last example (on the right).

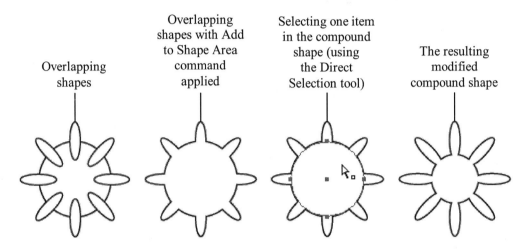

Exhibit 2-13: An example of how to create and manipulate compound shapes

If you are working with the Selection tool, you can temporarily access the Direct Selection tool by pressing Ctrl. To return to the Selection tool, release Ctrl. To select multiple items in a compound shape, press Ctrl+Shift and click the items you want to select.

Duplicating parts of a compound shape

Earlier, you learned to duplicate shapes either by copying and pasting, or by pressing Alt and dragging a shape. You can use the same techniques to duplicate specific parts of a compound shape. However, if you press Alt to duplicate a shape in a compound shape, the duplicate shape will be included in the compound shape. If you want to duplicate part of a compound shape but do not want the duplicate shape to be included in the compound shape, you must use the copy and paste method.

Do it!

C-4: Using the Add to Shape Area command

Do it!

Here's how	Here's why
ACE objective 2.15 1 Scroll so that the overlapping ellipse shapes are visible	(If necessary.) You'll use simple shapes to create a compound shape that looks like a spice shaker.
2 Create a new rectangle that is **1.25** inches wide and **.25** inches tall	Select the Rectangle tool and click once in the artboard to open the Rectangle dialog box.
3 Position the new rectangle so that it overlaps the two ellipses, as shown	 You'll need to select the Selection tool to position the shape.
4 Select the two ellipse shapes and the rectangle	Press Shift and click the two ellipses to select them, or drag to select all three shapes.
5 Choose **Window**, **Pathfinder**	To open the Pathfinder panel.
Tell students to move the pathfinder panel if necessary. 6 Under Shape Modes, click	The Add to shape area button.
Deselect the shapes	The compound shape looks like one object, but still consists of three shapes.
7 In the Tools panel, click	The Direct Selection tool.
8 Click the center of the compound shape	To select just the rectangle.
Drag the rectangle to the left	So that it is centered between the two ellipse shapes.
9 Using the arrow keys, nudge the rectangle into position until the shape looks similar to the example here	 This creates the top portion of the shaker.
Deselect the shape	
10 Using the Selection tool, create a duplicate of the compound shape	Press Alt and drag the compound shape to the right.

11 From the scratch area, move the rectangle to the artboard so that it overlaps the original compound shape, as shown

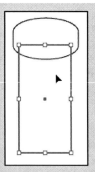

The rectangle creates the middle portion of the shaker.

Position the duplicate compound shape so that it overlaps the bottom of the rectangle, as shown

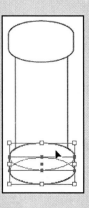

Before you combine the shapes, you'll horizontally align them.

12 Select both compound shapes and the rectangle

Press Shift and click the rectangle and the top compound shape, or drag to select all three shapes.

13 Observe the Control panel

With mixed shapes, the align buttons are visible directly in the panel.

In the Control panel, click

(The Horizontal Align Center button.) The three shapes shift slightly so that they are horizontally aligned.

14 In the Pathfinder panel, click the Add to shape area button

To combine the shapes into a compound shape.

Deselect the compound shape

To view the results. You'll add an ellipse to the top of the spice shaker so that it looks more three-dimensional.

15 Use the Direct Selection tool to click the top of the spice shaker

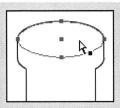

To select one of the ellipse shapes.

Remind students they need to copy and paste the ellipse so that it is not part of the compound shape.

Press (CTRL) + (C)

To copy the ellipse.

Press (CTRL) + (V)

To paste a duplicate of the ellipse.

16 Use the Selection tool to position the duplicate ellipse at the top of the spice shaker, as shown

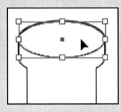

You'll reduce the size of the ellipse slightly.

Press (SHIFT) + (ALT) and resize the ellipse so that it is slightly smaller

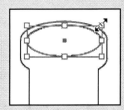

17 Deselect the ellipse

To view the results.

18 Close the Pathfinder panel

19 Update the document

Grouping shapes

Explanation

You might want to combine several shapes so they act as one unit, but you don't want to combine them to form a single shape (as is the case in compound shapes). By grouping shapes, you can move, resize, rotate, and even format them without having to select each shape individually.

To group shapes, select them and choose Object, Group (or press Ctrl+G). To select a group, click one of the shapes in the group by using the Selection tool. You can then move, scale, rotate, and arrange the group as you would arrange a single object. You can also combine this group with other shapes or groups. To ungroup shapes, select the group and choose Object, Ungroup (or press Shift+Ctrl+G).

Manipulating items within a group

Once items are grouped, there are several ways you can select and manipulate individual objects within the group. You can edit the group in isolation mode, or select and reposition objects using the Direct Selection and Group Selection tools.

Isolation mode

ACE objective 2.2

Isolation mode is a unique way to work with grouped objects without having to ungroup them. In isolation mode, any items in the drawing not included in the group are dimmed and locked, and the items within the group are treated as individual objects. The items are still grouped, however, you can manipulate them as if they weren't. Isolation mode is useful, for example, if you want to draw a new object and add it to the group. Instead of ungrouping the original objects, making the changes and additions, and then regrouping them, you can add the new object in Isolation mode, then quickly return to the illustration. When a group is isolated, any new shapes or objects that are created become part of the group. You can also use this technique to manipulate components within a compound shape.

To edit grouped items in isolation mode:

1 To enter isolation mode, do one of the following:

- Using the Selection tool, double-click an item within the group.
- Click to select the group, then click the Isolate Selected Group button in the Control panel.

All items not included in the group are dimmed and locked, and an isolation bar appears at the top of the work area, as shown in Exhibit 2-14.

2 Select, move, or otherwise manipulate the individual items in the group.

3 To exit isolation mode, do one of the following:

- Double-click outside of the isolated group.
- Click the Exit Isolation Group button in the isolation mode bar.
- Click the Exit Isolated Group button in the Control panel.

Exit Isolated Group button

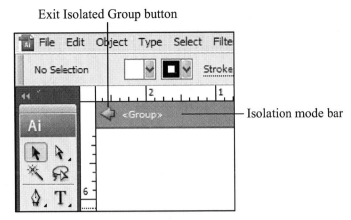

Isolation mode bar

Exhibit 2-14: The isolation mode bar

If several sets of grouped items are combined (nested) into a larger group, then double-clicking the group will allow you to manipulate each subgroup within the larger group. You can double-click a subgroup to individually manipulate the items within that subgroup.

Direct Selection tool

ACE objective 2.2

Another way to select and reposition grouped items is by using the Direct Selection tool. When you click an object within a group, you select only that object. However, you cannot alter the object the same way you can with the Selection tool. Specifically, the bounding box is not visible, so you cannot resize or skew the object unless you use the Transform panel. The Direct Selection tool is more useful when manipulating paths and anchor points, which is covered later in the course.

Group Selection tool

Another way to select and reposition grouped items is by using the Group Selection tool. The Group Selection tool selects an object within a group, a single group within multiple groups, or a set of groups within the artwork. For example, if you had two sets of grouped items that you then grouped together, you'd have a group made up of two subgroups. Using the Group Selection tool, you could use these techniques to select the items within the group:

- Click an individual object within either subgroup to select only that item.
- Click the item object just selected to add the rest of the items in its subgroup to the selection.
- Click any of the objects in the subgroup you just selected to add the items in the other subgroup to the selection.

You can also use the Group Selection tool to drag individual items and subgroups within a group.

C-5: Grouping shapes

Here's how	Here's why
1 Select all five stars at the bottom of the artboard	You'll group the stars so that they are easier to select.
2 Choose **Object**, **Group**	To group the stars.
Deselect the stars, and click one of the stars	All five stars are selected as a unit.
3 Double-click any of the stars	To isolate the group. You can now manipulate the stars as though there were not part of a group. Other objects in the drawing are dimmed and locked.
4 Click the circle shape in the large sun	Since you are in isolation mode, you cannot select it.
5 In the row of stars, click the second star from the left	To select only that star.
Drag the star down	To move it without moving any of the other stars in the group. You'll now move the entire group.
6 Double-click a blank area of the artboard	To exit isolation mode.
7 Drag any of the stars	To move the entire group.
8 Press (CTRL) + (Z) two times	To undo the steps, returning the stars to their previous positions without ungrouping them.
9 Double-click a blank area of the artboard	To exit isolation mode. You'll also group the overlapping star and circle shapes in the sun.
10 Select the overlapping star and circle shapes used to create the large sun	
Press (CTRL) + (G)	To group the shapes. You'll also group the spice shaker and the ellipse at the top of the shaker.
11 Select the ellipse at the top of the spice shaker, and the compound spice shaker shape	
12 Group the shapes	Press Ctrl+G.
13 Deselect the spice shaker	
14 Update the document	

Rotating shapes

Explanation

ACE objective 2.3

You can choose from several ways to rotate shapes. The following table describes the available methods.

Method	Used to...	Description
Selection tool	Quickly rotate a shape around its center	Select the shape so that its bounding box is visible. (Choose View, Show Bounding Box, if necessary.) Point anywhere near the bounding box until the pointer changes to a curve with arrowheads at both ends. Drag in a circular motion to rotate the shape. You can also press Shift as you drag to restrict the rotation to increments of 45°.
Rotate tool	Rotate a shape around any point	Select the shape and then select the Rotate tool. Drag the shape to rotate it around its center. To rotate the shape around a point other than the center, click to specify the reference point and drag in a circular motion.
Rotate dialog box	Rotate at a specific angle or rotate a copy of the shape	Select the shape and double-click the Rotate tool to open the Rotate dialog box. Enter the angle of rotation in the Angle box and click OK. To rotate a copy of the shape, click Copy.
Control panel	Rotate at a specific angle	Select the shape, and expand the Transform drop-down panel. In the Angle box, enter the amount of rotation you want, and press Enter.

Reset the bounding box

When you rotate a shape by using the Selection tool, the bounding box for the shape rotates as well. You might want to reset the bounding box so that it looks the way it did before you rotated it. To do this, choose Object, Transform, Reset Bounding Box.

Do it!

C-6: Rotating shapes

ACE objective 2.3

Here's how	Here's why
1 Create a duplicate of the spice shaker and position it as shown	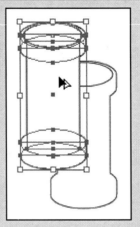
	(Move it up and to the left.) You'll rotate the duplicate shaker so that it tilts to the left.
2 Point just above the top-right handle of the selected shaker	The pointer changes to show two arrows pointing down and to the left.
	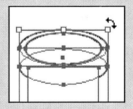
With the rotation arrows visible, drag slowly to the left	To begin rotating the shape.
3 Rotate the spice shaker so that it tilts to the left, as shown	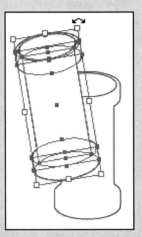
	You'll create a second duplicate shaker and tilt it in the opposite direction.

4 Create a second duplicate of the vertical shaker, and position it as shown

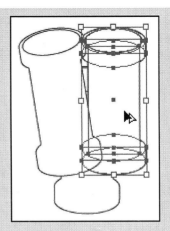

5 Rotate the spice shaker so that it tilts to the right

6 Deselect the shaker

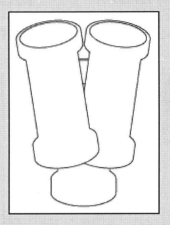

To view the results.

7 Update the document

Adjusting stacking order

Explanation

Shapes are stacked in the order in which you create them, which might hide some shapes as you create them. For example, if you create a small circle and then create a larger rectangle, the circle might be partially (or completely) behind the rectangle if they overlap. You can adjust the stacking order of shapes to bring them forward or send them backward. To do this, choose one of the four commands in the Object, Arrange submenu. The following table describes the commands.

Command	Shortcut	Description
Bring to Front	Shift+Ctrl+]	Positions a shape in front of all others in an illustration.
Bring Forward	Ctrl+]	Positions a shape one level above its current position in the stacking order.
Send Backward	Ctrl+[	Positions a shape one level below its current position in the stacking order.
Send to Back	Shift+Ctrl+[	Positions a shape behind all others.

Align to artboard

In addition to the basic align commands in the Align panel, you can also align objects in reference to the artboard, or to a crop area. You can do this using the Align to Artboard/Crop Area button in either the Align panel or the Control panel, as shown in Exhibit 2-15.

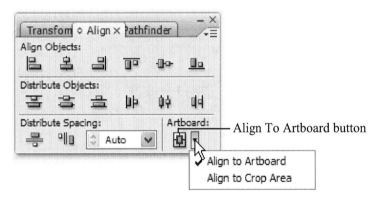

Exhibit 2-15: The Align to Artboard option in the Align panel

ACE objective 2.3

To align objects in reference to the artboard:

1 Select the objects you want to align.
2 In the Align panel or Control panel, expand the Align To Artboard menu, and verify that Align To Artboard is selected.
3 Click the Align to Artboard button to align the objects.

C-7:   Adjusting stacking order

Here's how	Here's why
1 Select the two tilting spice shakers	You'll adjust the stacking order of the shakers so that they are behind the vertical shaker.
2 Press CTRL + I	(Or choose Object, Arrange, Send Backward.) To move the shakers behind the vertical shaker.
Deselect the shapes	To see the results.
3 Select and group all three spice shakers	(Press Ctrl+G to group the selected shakers.) To finish the illustration, you'll align and reposition the grouped shapes.
4 Select the grouped stars, spice shakers, and the large sun	
5 In the Control panel, click the Horizontal Align Center button	
6 Click the Vertical Align Center button	You'll reposition the stars and bring them forward in the stacking order so that they are in front of the large sun.
7 Deselect the shapes, and select the grouped stars	The stars will only be partially visible behind the other objects.
8 Press CTRL + SHIFT + I	(Or choose Object, Arrange, Bring to Front.) To bring the stars to the front of the stacking order.
9 Drag the row of stars down toward the bottom of the spice shakers	
	Press Shift after you start dragging to keep the stars aligned.
Deselect the stars	To view the results.
10 Press CTRL + A	To select all the artwork.
11 Press CTRL + G	To group the objects.
12 In the Control panel, click the Align To Artboard button	Basic alignment and distribution options become visible.

Remind students the keyboard shortcut is for the Object, Arrange, Send Backward command.

⚠ *Make sure students click the Horizontal Align Center button and not the Horizontal Distribute button by mistake.*

Remind students the keyboard shortcut is for the Object, Arrange, Bring to Front command.

ACE objective 2.3

13 In the Control panel, click the Horizontal Align Center button	
Click the Vertical Align Center button	To position the artwork in the center of the artboard.
14 Update the document	

Topic D: Export an illustration

This topic covers the following ACE exam objectives for Illustrator CS3.

#	Objective
6.2	Explain how to apply metadata and keywords to assets in Adobe Bridge.
8.1	Given a file type, describe the options available when exporting an Illustrator document to that file type.
8.3	Describe the differences, and explain criteria for when you would output an Illustrator document to various file formats. (Formats include: PSD, EPS, PDF, SVG.)

Exporting Illustrator files

Explanation

Many types of documents created in Illustrator are used in newsletters, brochures, and other types of documents. Page layout programs are often used to create multi-page documents. While some of these programs can use native Illustrator files, not all of them can. It is helpful to export Illustrator files to formats that can be more widely used, such as TIFF and EPS files. In addition, to aid with cataloging the document, you might want to add metadata such as brief descriptive keywords.

Metadata

If you plan to share a document with others, or expect that you'll need to find it yourself later from among many files, you might find it helpful to add *metadata*, or additional information about the document such as keywords and author information that is stored along with the image data. You or others can then use applications such as Adobe Bridge or other image catalog programs to view and search on the metadata.

You can add metadata to an individual open file in Illustrator, or to multiple selected files at once in Bridge without opening them. To add or edit metadata in Illustrator, choose File, File Info. Click a category on the left side of the dialog box and enter information in the appropriate boxes. If the document is intended for use with news media, enter information in the categories beginning with IPTC, which contain metadata in a form standardized by the International Press Telecommunications Council. Go to www.newscodes.com for more information on IPTC metadata.

Illustrator documents retain metadata, as do files you save in formats that support it, such as TIFF and JPEG. However, because metadata adds to an image's file size, Illustrator strips away metadata in images saved with the Save for Web command in order to generate the smallest files possible.

Do it!

D-1:   Adding metadata in Illustrator

Here's how	Here's why
1 Choose **File**, **File Info...**	To open a dialog box into which you can enter metadata.
2 In the Document Title box, enter **Drawing of spice shakers**	To enter a descriptive title.
3 In the Author box, enter **Outlander Spices**	
4 In the Description box, enter **Drawing of shakers, to be used on a spice label**	
5 In the Keywords box, enter **shaker, label, shapes**	To add descriptive words that can be used to search for the document.
6 Click **OK**	To return to the image.
7 Update and close the document	

⚠ *Ensure students close this document because in the next activity they'll apply a keyword to it in Bridge, and you can't apply keywords in Bridge to an open document.*

Metadata in Adobe Bridge

Explanation

ACE objective 6.2

In addition to editing metadata for an individual open document in Illustrator, you can add it to multiple selected documents at once in Adobe Bridge without opening them. To add metadata in Adobe Bridge, select one or more documents, and either choose File, File Info, or enter data directly in the Metadata or Keywords tab.

If you select a document, its keywords appear in italics under Other Keywords at the bottom of the Keywords tab, and remain there until you close Bridge. This allows you to easily select another document and check keywords that appear, in order to apply them to other images.

If you want a keyword to remain in the Keywords tab permanently after you close and re-open Bridge, either create it by clicking the New Keyword button at the bottom of the Keywords tab, or right-click an existing italicized keyword and choose Make Persistent.

Do it!

D-2: Adding metadata in Bridge

ACE objective 6.2

Here's how	Here's why
1 In the Control panel, click	To open Adobe Bridge.
2 Activate the Folders tab	If necessary.
3 Navigate to the current unit folder	
Select **Chicken recipe card**	
4 Choose **File, File Info...**	To open the dialog box for entering metadata.
5 In the Author box, enter **<your name>**	
6 In the Keywords box, enter **chicken, recipe, spices**	
Click **OK**	
7 Activate the Metadata tab	(If necessary.) To display existing metadata.
8 Expand IPTC Core	(If necessary.) To expand it, click the triangle to the left of IPTC Core.
Observe the available options	Notice that the information you entered appears in the Creator and Keywords boxes.
9 Activate the Keywords tab	
Scroll down to the bottom	The keywords for the Chicken recipe card document appear in italics, indicating that they will disappear when Bridge is closed and re-opened, and checked, meaning that they're applied to the selected file.

Ask students to make the Metadata panel wider, if necessary.

10 Select **Spice shaker illustration**	
11 Scroll down to view its keywords	The keyword spices should also apply to the Spice shaker illustration file but are not checked.
12 Under Other Keywords, check **spices**	You work with Outlander spices frequently, so you'll make this keyword persistent so it always appears in Adobe Bridge.
13 Right-click **spices**	
Choose **Make Persistent**	The word no longer appears italicized, meaning that it will remain in Bridge even after it is closed and re-opened.
	You'll also add a persistent keyword for Outlander.
14 Click [icon]	(The New Keyword button, under the Keywords tab.) To add a new keyword.
15 Type **Outlander**	
Press (↵ ENTER)	You'll apply this keyword to both the Spice shaker illustration and Chicken recipe card documents.
16 Hold (CTRL) and click **Chicken recipe card**	To select the two files at once.
17 Check **Outlander**	(To apply it to the files.) A warning box opens.
Check **Don't show again** and click **Yes**	

	To continue. You'll also apply the same creator and copyright information to both Outlander illustrations.
18 Activate the Metadata tab	
On the Metadata tab, scroll down	To view the Copyright Notice.

19 To the right of Copyright Notice, click in the box as shown

Enter **Copyright 2008 Outlander Spices**

20 Edit the Creator box to read **Outlander Spices**   (Scroll to the top of the list.)

21 Click   To apply the metadata to the selected files.

22 Close Adobe Bridge   To return to Illustrator.

Export file formats

Explanation

ACE objective 8.1
ACE objective 8.3

TIFF and EPS formats are two of the most common export formats. The TIFF and EPS formats are compatible with most page layout, word processing, and graphics applications. The EPS format preserves most of the objects in your illustration, so you can reopen and edit EPS files. EPS files can contain both vector and raster graphics. TIFF files are rasterized graphics. If you need to edit an image that has been exported in TIFF format, you need to open the original Illustrator file to make the changes.

Format	Description
Enhanced Metafile (EMF), and Windows Metafile (WMF)	Use with Windows applications. Wherever possible, use the EMF format; the WMF format has limited vector graphics support.
EPS	Use to exchange vector or raster graphics between applications and computer platforms. Widely supported by page layout applications.
Macintosh PICT	Use in Macintosh graphics and page layout applications.
Macromedia Flash (SWF)	Use the Flash file on the Web or edit further in Flash.
CAD Formats	Use the AutoCAD drawing (DWG) and AutoCAD Interchange Files (DXF) for compatibility with drafting applications.
Photoshop (PSD)	Use to create a Photoshop file. Layers, masks, transparency, compound shapes, slices, image maps, and editable type when possible are preserved.
TIFF	Use to exchange raster graphic files between applications and computer platforms. Widely supported by image editing and page layout applications.
BMP	Use with Windows applications. BMP is a standard Windows raster image format.
Targa	Use with the Truevision® video board.
JPEG, GIF, and PNG	Use either the Export or Save for Web commands to create these Web graphic file types.
PDF	Use to share files with others who might not have Illustrator installed on their machines, or as an alternative format for commercial printing. Once you've created a PDF file, anyone with Adobe Acrobat Reader, which is available for free from www.adobe.com, can open and print it. PDFs are versatile in that they generally produce small file sizes, are platform-independent, and are editable (with the use of Adobe Acrobat). Also, PDFs can be reopened in Illustrator without any data loss.

Export an illustration

To export an illustration:

1. Choose File, Export to open the Export dialog box.
2. In the File name box, enter a name for the file. By default, the current name of the Illustrator document is visible.
3. From the Save as type list, choose a format for the document (as shown in Exhibit 2-16).
4. Click Save. Depending on the format, a dialog box with options for the format might appear.
5. If necessary, in the dialog box, select the appropriate export options and click OK.

Exhibit 2-16: The Export dialog box

Export an illustration to EPS

ACE objective 8.3

Some formats, such as EPS and PDF, are not available in the Save as type list in the Export dialog box. To export an Illustrator document to EPS or PDF format, you need to save the file in that format.

To export an illustration to EPS:

1. Choose File, Save As to open the Save As dialog box.
2. In the File name box, enter a name for the file. By default, the current name of the Illustrator document is visible.
3. From the Save as type list, choose Illustrator EPS (.EPS).
4. Click Save. The EPS Options dialog box appears.
5. Select the appropriate export options, and click OK.

D-3: Exporting an illustration

Here's how	Here's why
1 Open Spice shaker illustration	
2 Choose **File**, **Export...**	To open the Export dialog box. You'll export the illustration as a TIFF file.
From the Save as type list, choose **TIFF (*.TIF)**	
Navigate to the current unit folder and click **Save**	The TIFF Options dialog box appears.
3 Under Resolution, verify that **High** is selected	This ensures a high-quality image for printing.
Under Byte Order, verify that **IBM PC** is selected	
Clear **Embed ICC Profile**	(If necessary.) You do not want the profile to be embedded in the exported file.
Click **OK**	The file is exported as a TIFF file. You'll also export the illustration as an EPS file so that it can be edited without having to revert to the original Illustrator file, if necessary.
4 Choose **File**, **Save As...**	To open the Save As dialog box.
From the Save as type list, select **Illustrator EPS (*.EPS)**	
Navigate to the current unit folder and click **Save**	The EPS Options dialog box appears.
5 Under Preview, verify that **TIFF (8-bit Color)** is selected	
Click **OK**	The file is exported in the EPS format. Note also that the newly saved file is open in Illustrator.
6 Close the document	

Unit summary: Creating a simple illustration

Topic A   In this topic, you learned how to **create and save a new document**.

Topic B   In this topic, you learned how to **draw basic shapes**. You used some of the shape tools, and you learned how to **manipulate shapes as you draw them**. You also learned how to **draw shapes precisely**.

Topic C   In this topic, you learned how to **manipulate existing shapes**. This included scaling, rotating, aligning, and distributing shapes. You also learned how to combine simple shapes to **make a compound shape**.

Topic D   In this topic, you learned how to **export** an illustration to several common formats.

Independent practice activity

In this activity, you'll create a new print document, and use basic shapes to create a complex compound shape. In the process, you'll duplicate, scale, rotate, and align shapes to create the end result. Lastly, you'll export the artwork as a TIFF file.

1 Create a new document that uses the Print preset. Verify the document uses inches for the unit of measure and the CMYK color mode. Title the new document **Recipe practice** and verify the Landscape orientation option is selected.

2 Save the new document in the current unit folder as **Recipe practice**.

3 Using basic shapes, create a compound shape similar to the example in Exhibit 2-17. (*Hint*: Create three circles and two thin rectangles. Overlap the shapes as shown, and click the Add to shape area button in the Pathfinder panel. Use the Direct Selection tool to nudge the shapes into position if necessary.)

4 Create two duplicates of the compound shape; then rotate and position the shapes similar to the example in Exhibit 2-18. (*Hint*: Select the two horizontal shapes, and press Ctrl+Shift+[to send them to the back of the stacking order.)

5 Create an additional duplicate of the vertical compound shape, then scale the shape proportionally so that it is approximately one inch wide. (*Hint*: To make scaling the shape easier, view the rulers and the artboard grid. To scale the shape proportionally, press Shift and drag one of the corner bounding box handles.)

6 Create four more duplicates of the scaled compound shape, then align and evenly distribute the shapes similar to the example in Exhibit 2-18. (*Hint*: To align and distribute the shapes, use the options available in the Align panel.)

7 If necessary, reposition the entire illustration so that it is centered on the artboard.

8 Export the illustration as a TIFF file to the current unit folder.

9 Update and close the document.

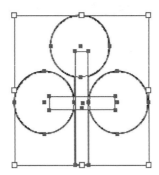

Exhibit 2-17: The compound shape after completing step 3 in the Independent practice activity

Exhibit 2-18: The illustration after completing step 6 in the Independent practice activity

Review questions

1 If you're creating a document intended for commercial printing, you should typically use which color mode: RGB or CMYK?

CMYK

2 When saving an Illustrator file, which are options available in the Illustrator Options dialog box? (Choose all that apply.)

   A Create a PDF-compatible file

   B Include color swatches

   C Include linked files

   D Embed ICC Profiles

3 You are saving an illustration and have the Illustrator Options dialog box visible. What is the benefit of checking the Create PDF Compatible File box?

   A It makes the document compatible with other Adobe applications.

   B It creates a PDF of the file instead of saving it in the native Illustrator format.

   C It creates an additional PDF file you can open and view in Acrobat Reader.

   D It makes the document compatible with earlier versions of Illustrator.

4 Which options are available in the Document Setup dialog box? (Choose all that apply.)

   A Artboard size

   B Default font

   C Grid size and color

   D Unit of measurement

5 You have the Document Setup dialog box open and you want to set the size of the artboard to 9 inches by 12 inches. You should:

   A Choose 9x12 from the Size list.

   B Choose Custom from the Size list to open the Size dialog box, and then enter the values you want.

   C Change the values in the Width and Height boxes to the size you want.

   D Choose Inches from the Units list; then choose Custom from the Size list to open the Size dialog box, and enter the values you want.

6 Pressing which key as you draw an ellipse constrains it to a circle?

   A Ctrl

   B Alt

   C Shift

   D Caps Lock

7 True or false? Clicking within a document with a shape tool opens a dialog box in which you can enter numeric size values for the new shape.

True

8 Which are ways you can scale an existing shape? (Choose all that apply.)

A Select a shape with the Selection tool and drag a handle on its bounding box.

B Select a shape with the Selection tool, and then double-click the shape to open the Scale dialog box and enter the size values you want.

C Select the Scale tool and drag on the artboard.

D Enter size values in the Control panel.

9 How can you select two or more shapes in an illustration? (Choose all that apply.)

A Using the Selection tool, click the shapes you want to select.

B Using the Selection tool, click a shape to select it; then press Shift and click the additional shapes you want to select.

C Using the Direct Selection tool, click the shapes you want to select.

D Using the Lasso tool, drag around all or part of the shapes you want to select.

10 Pressing which key as you drag a selected item with the Selection tool duplicates it?

A Ctrl

B Alt

C Shift

D Caps Lock

11 Which Shape Mode command creates a compound shape based on the outer boundaries of two or more selected shapes?

A Intersect Shape Areas

B Subtract From Shape Area

C Add To Shape Area

D Exclude Overlapping Shape Areas

12 How can you reposition an individual component of a compound shape? (Choose all that apply.)

A Using the Direct Selection tool, drag the component you want to reposition.

B Using the Selection tool, press Shift and click on the component you want to reposition to select it; then drag to reposition it.

C Using the Selection tool, drag the component you want to reposition.

D Using the Selection tool, double-click the compound shape to isolate the group and drag to reposition the component.

13 How can you duplicate one component of a compound shape so that it is separate from the original compound shape?

   A Using the Direct Selection tool, press Alt and drag the component you want to duplicate.

   B Using the Selection tool, press Alt and drag the component you want to duplicate.

   C Using the Direct Selection tool, select the component you want to duplicate and copy and paste the component.

   D Using the Selection tool, select the component you want to duplicate and copy and paste the component.

14 Which tools can you use to select individual objects in a group? (Choose all the apply.)

   A Selection tool

   B Direct Selection tool

   C Group Selection tool

   D Magic Wand tool

15 How can you select an individual object in a group by using the Selection tool?

   A Click directly on the border of the object you want to select in the group.

   B Press Ctrl and click on the object you want to select in the group.

   C Right-click the object in the group you want to select, and then choose Select Object.

   D Double-click the group to isolate it, then click the object you want to select.

16 Which statements about adding metadata to files in Adobe Bridge are true? (Choose all that apply.)

   A You can add metadata to an individual open file in Illustrator, or to multiple selected files at once in Bridge without opening them.

   B Metadata added to Illustrator files remain when you save the file for the Web by using the Save for Web command.

   C If an Illustrator file is intended for use with news media, you can enter metadata information in the categories beginning with IPTC, which contain a form standardized by the International Press Telecommunications Council

   D Metadata is a good way to share information about Illustrator files should you be working in a group environment.

17 You have several files selected in Adobe Bridge and you want to add the same metadata information to them all simultaneously. You should:

A Choose Edit, Selection, and then enter the information you want in the corresponding boxes.

B Double-click one of the selected files to open the dialog box for entering metadata, and then enter the information you want in the corresponding boxes.

C Choose File, File Info to open the dialog box for entering metadata, and then enter the information you want in the corresponding boxes.

D Choose View, As Details to view the current details for the selected files, and then enter the information you want in the corresponding boxes next to each file.

18 You have an illustration that you want to place in a page layout application, but you also want to be able to edit the artwork later on should you need to. Which file type would be most appropriate?

A GIF

B JPEG

C TIFF

D EPS

19 Which options are available when you export an Illustrator document as a TIFF? (Choose all that apply.)

A Setting the color model to use (RGB, CMYK, or Grayscale)

B Determining whether or not to embed fonts

C Determining whether or not to embed ICC profiles

D Determining the image resolution

20 How can you export an illustration as an EPS file?

A Choose File, Export, and then choose Illustrator EPS from the Format list.

B Choose File, Export, and then enter the name you want for the file followed by the extension .eps.

C Choose File, Save As, and then choose Illustrator EPS from the Format list.

D Choose File, Save As, and then enter the name you want for the file followed by the extension .eps.

21 Which file types are generally better when saving artwork for the Web? (Choose all that apply.)

A GIF

B TIFF

C JPEG

D PNG

Unit 3

Applying basic color

Unit time: 50 minutes

Complete this unit, and you'll know how to:

A Use the Swatches panel and the Color panel to apply color to shapes, and store new colors in the Swatches panel.

B Set basic stroke attributes for shapes, and create a dashed line effect.

C Use the Eyedropper tool to sample colors and apply them to shapes.

Topic A: Apply color

This topic covers the following ACE exam objectives for Illustrator CS3.

#	Objective
3.2	Apply colors, strokes, fills, and gradients to objects by using the Fill box, Stroke box, or Appearance panel.
3.3	List and describe the functionality of the Color Guide panel. (Functionality includes: color harmony rules, panel options, color groups.)

Fill and stroke

Explanation

As you create illustrations, you'll usually want to incorporate color into them. At its simplest level, you can apply color to the fill and stroke of each shape or path. The term *fill* refers to the color of the area inside the outline of a shape, and the term *stroke* refers to the color of its outline, as shown in Exhibit 3-1. You can use different color modes to define the fill and stroke colors. Color modes, such as CMYK or RGB, define the process by which colors are created for printing and displaying on a screen. You apply color to items by using the Swatches and Color panels.

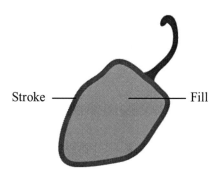

Exhibit 3-1: An example of the fill and stroke attributes of an item

Fill and stroke options in the Tools panel

ACE objective 3.2

To determine whether you apply a color to either the stroke or fill of an item, you need to select the Fill or Stroke icons in the Tools panel or the Color panel. Exhibit 3-2 shows the fill and stroke options available at the bottom of the Tools panel.

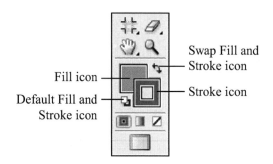

Exhibit 3-2: The fill and stroke options in the Tools panel

You can perform the following actions using the fill and stroke options in the Tools panel:

- To define the fill color of an object, click the Fill icon so it overlaps the Stroke icon.
- To define the stroke of an object, click the Stroke icon so it overlaps the Fill icon.
- To swap the current fill and stroke colors, click the Swap Fill and Stroke icon.
- To revert to the default fill and stroke colors, which is black for stroke and white for fill, click the Default Fill and Stroke icon.

The Swatches panel

The Swatches panel contains predefined color tiles called swatches. *Swatches* are an assorted collection of colors, gradients, and patterns that you can apply to your artwork. By default, the Swatches panel shows all the preset swatches available. This includes basic color swatches, gradient swatches, and pattern swatches, as shown in Exhibit 3-3. You can point to each swatch in the panel to see its name. In the top-left corner is the None swatch, which you can click to remove color from the selected item. Some color swatches have small white triangles in their lower-right corner. This indicates that the color is a global color, which, if updated, updates all instances of the color within your artwork.

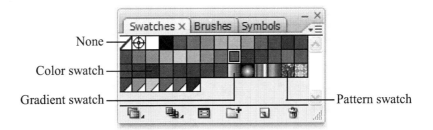

Exhibit 3-3: The Swatches panel

The Swatches panel also contains a series of buttons at the bottom that you can use to switch libraries, change how swatches appear in the panel, or to create and delete swatches.

The following table shows each button and its function.

Button	Description
Swatch Libraries menu	Open other color swatch libraries included with Illustrator. For example, you can view primarily earthtone color swatches by selecting the Earthtone library from the menu list.
Show Swatch Kinds menu	Show or hide specific swatch types. For example, you can opt to show only gradient or pattern swatches.
Swatch Options	You can edit a color swatch by selecting it and clicking the Swatch Options button. When you do, the Swatch Options dialog box appears, within which you can make the changes.
New Color Group	You can create a new color group within the Swatches panel to store specific swatches. You can only group solid colors. Gradients and patterns cannot be grouped.
New Swatch	Create a new color swatch based on the color currently defined in the Color panel.
Delete Swatch	Delete a swatch.

To apply color to an item by using the Swatches panel:

1 Using the Selection tool, select the item you want to apply color to.

2 In either the Tools panel or the Color panel, click either the Fill or Stroke icon to specify whether you want to add a color to the fill or stroke.

3 In the Swatches panel, click one of the swatches.

The Color Guide panel

ACE objective 3.3

In addition to the colors in the Swatches panel, you can also use the Color Guide panel to select colors. The Color Guide panel automatically shows harmonious color suggestions based on the current active Fill or Stroke color in the Tools panel. For example, if you apply a blue fill color to an object, the Color Guide automatically shows color group suggestions based on the blue color. You can change the way the panel suggests colors by selecting a new harmony rule from the Harmony Rules list, as shown in the second example in Exhibit 3-4. You can also save a suggested group of colors to the Swatches panel by clicking the Save color group to Swatch panel button.

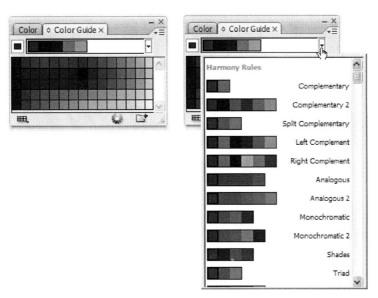

Exhibit 3-4: The Color Guide and the Color Guide with Harmony Rules list expanded

Show/Hide shape edges

Sometimes, as you apply color or manipulate shapes, you'll want to hide the edges of the shape so that you can better preview how it looks. This is especially true when working with compound shapes, because they include multiple shapes combined together, as shown in the first example (on the left) in Exhibit 3-5. To show/hide the edges of a shape, choose View, Hide Edges (or press Ctrl+H).

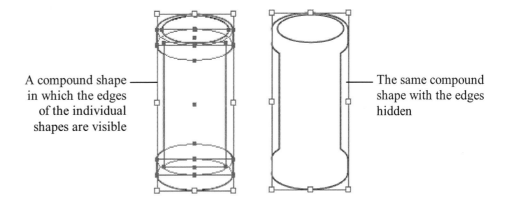

A compound shape in which the edges of the individual shapes are visible

The same compound shape with the edges hidden

Exhibit 3-5: An example of a compound shape with edges visible and hidden

Do it!

A-1: Using the Swatches panel

Here's how	Here's why
1 Open **Spice shaker illustration_color**	Located in the current unit folder.
Save the document as **My spice label illustration_color**	You'll begin adding color to the illustration by using some predefined color swatches.
2 In the panel dock, click ▦	(The Swatches icon.) To expand the Swatches panel.
3 In the panel, click ⬛	(The Show Swatch Kinds menu button.) To expand the list.
From the list, select **Show Color Swatches**	To view only the color swatches in the panel.
4 Using the Selection tool, double-click one of the spice shakers	To isolate the group.
5 Select the shaker that tilts to the left	
6 Press and hold ⌨CTRL + ⌨SHIFT	The pointer changes to the Direct Selection tool.
Click the ellipse at the top of the shaker	
	To deselect it.
7 In the Swatches panel, click the **Little Sprout Green** swatch	(To apply the color to the shaker.) Point to each green swatch to view the color name.
8 Press ⌨CTRL + ⌨H	To hide the edges of the compound shape and view the color better. You'll now remove the black stroke from the shaker.
9 In the Tools panel, click the Stroke icon, as shown	
	To make the stroke attribute active. When you click the Stroke icon in the Tools panel, it automatically expands the Color panel in the panel dock.
10 In the panel dock, click ▦	(The Swatches icon.) To expand the Swatches panel again.

Make sure students click inside the ellipse, not on the ellipse path. If students select the ellipse path, instruct them to click inside the ellipse until the ellipse is deselected.

TIPS *You can point to each swatch to view the color name.*

ACE objective 3.2

11	In the Swatches panel, click the **[None]** swatch	
		To remove the black stroke.
12	Press ⟨CTRL⟩ + ⟨H⟩	To view the edges of the shapes again.
	Click a blank area of the artboard	To deselect the spice shaker. Next, you'll remove the black stroke from the white ellipse at the top of the shaker.
Again, make sure students select the entire ellipse, not the ellipse path.	13 Press ⟨CTRL⟩ + ⟨SHIFT⟩, then click the ellipse at the top of the shaker	To select the ellipse.
	14 In the Swatches panel, click the **[None]** swatch	To remove the black stroke.
	Deselect the ellipse	(Click a blank area on the artboard.) To view the results.
	15 Update the document	Notice that when you update the document, you automatically exit isolation mode.

The Color panel

Explanation

You can add new colors to the Swatches panel. To create custom colors, you use the Color panel, shown in Exhibit 3-6.

To apply color to an object by using the Color panel:

1 Using the Selection tool, select the item you want to apply color to.
2 In the Color panel, select either the Fill or Stroke icon.
3 Choose a color.

- Select a color from the Color Spectrum bar. Point anywhere on the Color Spectrum bar and click to select a color.
- Create a color by dragging the color sliders, or entering values in the percentage boxes until the desired color is created.

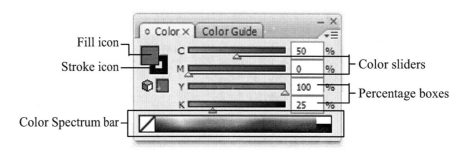

Exhibit 3-6: The Color panel

By default, the Color panel shows color sliders and percentage boxes based on the color mode you selected when you created the document. For example, if you selected the CMYK color mode, the Color panel shows CMYK color sliders and percentage boxes. You can choose another color mode from the Color panel menu, shown in Exhibit 3-7. You can select Grayscale, RGB, HSB, CMYK, or Web Safe RGB.

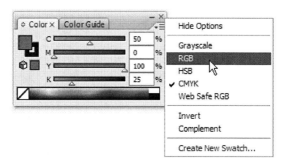

Exhibit 3-7: Selecting a different color mode

Using the Control panel to apply color

ACE objective 3.2

You can access the Swatches and Color panels by using the Control panel. To access the Swatches panel, click the small downward arrow to the right of the Fill or Stroke boxes, as shown in the first (left) example in Exhibit 3-8. To access the Color panel, press Shift and click the small downward arrow, as shown in the second (right) example.

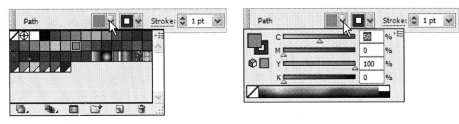

Exhibit 3-8: The Swatch and Color drop-down panels in the Control panel

A-2: Using the Color panel

Here's how	Here's why
1 Select the sun shape	(Use the Selection tool.) You'll create some custom colors for the sun.
2 Expand the Color panel	In the panel dock, click the Color icon.
3 Click the Fill icon as shown	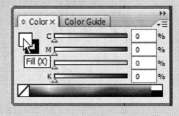
	To make the fill color active.
4 Point to a yellow area of the CMYK spectrum	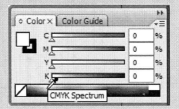
Click to select a yellow color	The yellow color fills both selected objects. You'll adjust the color by using the color sliders.
5 Drag the C, M, and K color sliders all the way to the left	(If necessary.) To set them to 0.
Drag the Y color slider to approximately **60**	To choose a light yellow color. You'll also remove the black stroke from the items.
	You can use the Control panel to remove the stroke without having to activate the Stroke icon.
6 In the Control panel, click the small downward arrow to the right of the Stroke swatch, as shown	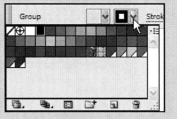
	To view the Swatches drop-down panel.
From the list of swatches, click the **[None]** swatch	To remove the black stroke. You'll make the center portion of the sun a brighter yellow.
7 Press (CTRL) + (SHIFT), then click the star portion of the sun shape	To deselect it.

Remind students that when they updated the document in the previous activity, it automatically exited isolation mode for the three spice shakers.

ACE objective 3.2

8 In the Colors panel, drag the M
   color slider to approximately **5**

   Drag the Y color slider to
   approximately **85**

9 Deselect the sun shape   (Click a blank area of the artboard.) To view the
                             results.

Storing colors

Explanation

After you define a color, you can save it as a swatch in the Swatches panel for easy access later. Colors you add to the Swatches panel are available only within the document you are using. They won't appear in the Swatches panel for other documents.

To store a new color in the Swatches panel:

1 Create the color you want in the Color panel.

2 In the Swatches panel, click the New Swatch button. The New Swatch dialog box appears, as shown in Exhibit 3-9. Alternatively, you can drag the color from the Colors panel to the Swatches panel. To open the New Swatch dialog box, you need to double-click the new color swatch in the Swatches panel.

3 In the Swatch Name box, enter a name for the new color, if necessary.

4 If you want instances of this color within your artwork to update if you edit the color, check Global.

5 Click OK.

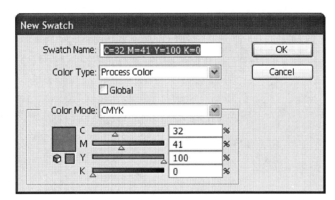

Exhibit 3-9: The New Swatch dialog box

Do it!   **A-3:   Storing colors**

Here's how	Here's why
1 Select the row of stars at the bottom of the illustration	You'll fill the stars with a custom gold color.
2 In the Color panel, in the C box, enter **32**	
In the M box, enter **41**	
In the Y box, enter **100** and press (↵ ENTER)	You'll store the color in the Swatches panel.
3 Expand the Swatches panel	
4 In the panel, click [⬛]	(The New Swatch button.) The New Swatch dialog box appears with the new color information in it. The swatch name shows the CMYK values.
5 In the Swatch Name box, change the title to **Gold**	
Click **OK**	To close the dialog box.
6 Observe the Swatches panel	To see that the new gold color is visible at the end of the swatches.
7 Remove the black stroke from the stars	In the Control panel, click the small downward arrow to the right of the Stroke swatch, then select the [None] color swatch.
8 Double-click one of the spice shakers	To isolate the group.
9 Select the center spice shaker	
Press (CTRL) + (SHIFT) and click the ellipse at the top of the shaker	To deselect it. You'll create and store a custom dark green color.
10 In the Swatches panel, click the Emerald swatch	To apply a green color to the shaker.
11 Expand the Color panel	
12 In the panel, in the K box, change the value to **40**, and press (↵ ENTER)	To make a darker green color.

13	Add the new dark green color to the Swatches panel as **Dark Green**	(Expand the Swatches panel, then click the New Swatch button. In the Name box, enter Dark Green and click OK.)
		You'll also remove the stroke formatting from the center spice shaker.
14	In the Tools panel, click the Stroke icon	To activate the stroke attribute for the shaker.
	Click the None icon	
		To remove the black stroke from the shaker. Lastly, you'll remove the stroke formatting for the ellipse at the top of the shaker.
15	Deselect the shaker	
16	Press (CTRL) + (SHIFT) and click the ellipse at the top of the shaker	To select the ellipse.
	Remove the black stroke	In the Tools panel, click the [None] icon.
17	Update the document	Again, when you update the document, you automatically exit isolation mode.

Remind students that they cannot use the Stroke drop-down panel (in the Control panel) for compound shapes.

Topic B: Stroke options

This topic covers the following ACE exam objective for Illustrator CS3.

#	Objective
2.5	Given a scenario, edit the stroke and/or fill attributes of an object. (Scenarios include: stroke alignment, overprinting, and dash patterns.)

Modifying stroke attributes

Explanation

You can use the Stroke panel to vary the thickness of the stroke, change the way it joins or appears at corner points, or make it appear as a dashed line.

Stroke attributes

Stroke weight is the thickness of an item's stroke. By default, if you apply a thick stroke weight to a path, it is evenly centered on the path, as shown in Exhibit 3-10. However, you can also vary how the stroke weight is aligned. The value for stroke weight can vary from 0 to 1000, where 0 means no stroke at all.

1 pt stroke ——————————   —— 7 pt stroke

Exhibit 3-10: An example of stroke thickness

ACE objective 2.5

To set basic stroke attributes for an item:

1   Select the object.

2   Expand the Stroke panel. You might need to choose Window, Stroke if the Stroke panel is not visible.

3   If necessary, view all the options in the panel by clicking the small triangles on the left side of the tab. Clicking the triangles shows three views of the panel. You can click several times to see the view you want.

4   In the Weight box, enter a value for the stroke weight, or select a value from the Weight list. You can also click the increment buttons on the left side of the Weight box to increase or decrease the stroke weight.

5   Select a cap button to determine how the end of an open path looks.

6   Select a join button to determine how the corner points for connected path segments look.

7   Next to Align Stroke, set how you want the stroke aligned to the path.

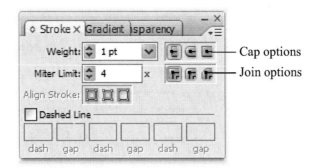

Cap options

Join options

Exhibit 3-11: The Stroke panel

Cap and Join options

On closely observing the beginning or end of a stroke, you can see that the stroked line appears to have rectangular edges at the end of the path. This is the *cap* of the stroke. You can change the cap options by selecting the path and clicking the appropriate button on the Stroke panel.

You can also define the *join* style for the corner anchor points that join two segments on a path. To vary the join options, select the path that has corner points and alter the join options of the stroke by clicking the appropriate button on the Stroke panel. The following table describes the buttons on the Stroke panel.

Button	Name	Description
	Butt Cap	Ends a stroke with a rectangular edge.
	Round Cap	Ends a stroke slightly beyond the path in a uniform rounded curve.
	Projecting Cap	Ends a stroke with a protruding rectangular edge, meaning the stroke ends beyond the end of the path up to a distance that is half the stroke weight.
	Miter Join	Converts corner points of joined segments to pointed corners.
	Round Join	Converts corner points of joined segments to rounded corners.
	Bevel Join	Converts corner points of joined segments to squared-off corners.

Align Stroke options

ACE objective 2.5

For closed paths, you can adjust the alignment of the stroke in relation to the path. You can choose to have the stroke appear along the outside or inside of the path, instead of being centered evenly on the path (as shown in Exhibit 3-10). The following table shows the three path alignment options available in the Stroke panel and examples of each.

Button	Name	Example
▣	Align Stroke to Center (default)	☆
▣	Align Stroke to Inside	☆
▣	Align Stroke to Outside	☆

Miter limit

The miter limit controls when Illustrator changes from a mitered (pointed) join to a beveled (squared-off) join. The default miter limit is 4, which means that when the length of the point reaches four times the stroke weight, the program switches from a miter join to a bevel join. A miter limit of 1 results in a bevel join.

Do it!

B-1: Setting basic stroke attributes

Here's how	Here's why
1 Select the row of stars at the bottom of the illustration	You'll change the appearance of the stars so that they are white with gold outlines.
2 In the Color panel, click the Fill icon	To activate the fill.
3 To the right of the Spectrum bar, click the white swatch, as shown	
4 In the Color panel, click the Stroke icon	To activate the stroke attributes for the stars.
5 In the Control panel, expand the Stroke color drop-down panel Click the Gold swatch	Click the small downward arrow to the right of the Stroke swatch. To create a thin stroke of gold around the stars.
6 Press (CTRL) + (H)	To hide the edges of the grouped shapes and view the color better. You'll make the stroke more prominent.
7 In the panel group, click [≡]	(The Stroke icon.) To expand the Stroke panel.
8 From the Weight list, select **5 pt**	To make the stroke thicker. You'll also align the stroke to the outside of the star shapes.
9 In the panel tab, click the [◊] icon twice	 (The icon is located to the left of the tab name.) The panel first contracts, then expands to show all the panel options.
10 In the Align Stroke section, click [□]	(The Align Stroke to Outside button.) Lastly, you'll make the edges of the stroke more round.
11 Click [⌐]	The Round Join button.

Remind students that they can also make these selections from the Stroke and Stroke Weight drop-down panels in the Control panel.

ACE objective 2.5

12 Press CTRL + H	To view the edges of the stars again.
	You'll also add a dark green border around the light green spice shaker.
13 Double-click one of the spice shakers	To isolate the group.
14 Select the light green spice shaker	The shaker that's leaning toward the left.
Press CTRL + SHIFT and click the ellipse at the top of the shaker	To deselect it.
In the Tools panel, verify that the Stroke icon is selected	
15 Expand the Swatches panel, then click the Dark Green swatch	To apply a thin dark green border.
16 Set the stroke to 5 pts	(Expand the Stroke panel, then select 5 pt from the Weight list.)
	Lastly, you'll apply a thick white stroke to the circle in the sun shape.
17 In the Isolation bar, click the Exit Isolated Group button	
	To exit isolation mode.
18 Press CTRL and select the circle in the sun shape	Make sure to select the circle, not the star portion of the sun shape.
19 Apply a 10-pt white stroke to the circle	In the Swatches panel, click the White swatch. In the Stroke panel, from the Weight list, select 10 pt.
20 Deselect the circle, and update the document	

Creating dashed lines

Explanation

ACE objective 2.5

You can make parts of the stroke invisible, giving it a dashed look. To create a dashed line, check Dashed Line on the Stroke panel, then enter values in the dash and gap boxes, as shown in Exhibit 3-12. The default value for the first box is 12 points, which gives the stroke a uniform dashed look. You can create a pattern of varying dash and gap lengths by entering different values in the dash and gap boxes.

To remove the dashed stroke and revert to the normal stroke, select the path that has the dashed stroke and clear Dashed Line in the Stroke panel.

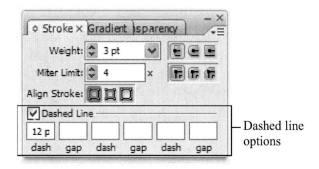

Exhibit 3-12: Dashed line options in the Stroke panel

Do it!

B-2:   Creating a dashed line

Here's how	Here's why
1 Double-click one of the spice shakers	To isolate the group.
2 Select the ellipse at the top of the light green spice shaker	(Press Ctrl and click the ellipse.) You'll make the ellipse at the top of the spice shaker appear as a set of holes.
3 In the Swatches panel, click the Black swatch	(You'll need to expand the Swatches panel.) To apply a thin black stroke.
4 Press (CTRL) + (H)	To hide the edges of the shape.
5 In the Stroke panel, from the Weight list, select **3 pt**	(You'll need to expand the Stroke panel.) To create a prominent black stroke. You'll use a dashed line to create the holes.
6 In the Stroke panel, check **Dashed Line**	
7 In the left-most dash box, change the value to **1** In the left-most gap box, enter **5**, and press (↵ ENTER)	

ACE objective 2.5

Align Stroke: ☐ ☐ ☐
☑ Dashed Line
1 pt	5 pt		
dash	gap	dash	gap

The ellipse now is a dotted line, but the dots do not look like shaker holes.

8 Click ⬅	(The Round Cap button.) To round the corners of the dashes.
9 In the Color panel, in the K box, enter **50**, and press (↵ ENTER)	You'll need to expand the Color panel.
10 Press (CTRL) + (H)	To view the edges of the shape again.

Topic C: The Eyedropper tool

Explanation

After applying fill and stroke attributes to an item, you might want to apply the same attributes to other objects. You can do so by using the Eyedropper tool.

To copy attributes by using the Eyedropper tool:

1   In the Tools panel, select the Eyedropper tool.

2   Use either of these techniques to copy attributes from one object and apply them to other objects:

- Press Ctrl to temporarily access the Selection tool and select the item(s) that will have the attributes applied. Release Ctrl to return to the Eyedropper tool and click the item whose attributes you want to copy. The attributes are now applied to the selected item(s).

- Click the item whose attributes you want to copy. Press Alt to change the mouse pointer to a filled eyedropper, and click to apply the attributes to the desired items. The initial click samples the attributes and "holds" them within the eyedropper, so you can apply them to multiple items. And, those items don't have to be selected prior to Alt-clicking.

To define the attributes that the Eyedropper tool picks up, double-click the Eyedropper or Paint Bucket tool. The Eyedropper/Paint Bucket options dialog box opens, and you can check or clear the options that you want these tools to copy and apply.

Using the Eyedropper tool, you can also copy RGB colors from anywhere on the desktop or any other application. To do so, after selecting an item in Illustrator, point anywhere in the document window, then press the mouse button and drag to the object outside Illustrator. Release the mouse button when the color attributes are visible in the Fill and Stroke boxes of the Tools panel.

Do it!   ## C-1: Using the Eyedropper tool

Here's how	Here's why
1 Select the white spice shaker	(The spice shaker tilting to the right.)(You should still be in isolation mode.)
	You'll use the Eyedropper tool to quickly format the shaker.
2 Deselect the ellipse at the top of the shaker	Press Ctrl+Shift and click the ellipse.
3 In the Tools panel, click [eyedropper icon]	The Eyedropper tool.
4 Point to the light green spice shaker	The spice shaker tilting to the left.
Click once	The light green fill and the dark green stroke are applied to the right spice shaker. You'll also use the Eyedropper tool to format the ellipses at the top of the shakers so that they are all the same.
5 Press ⬚CTRL⬚ and click a blank area of the artboard	(To deselect the spice shaker.) Pressing Ctrl temporarily accesses the Selection tool.
6 In the Tools panel, select the Direct Selection tool	
7 Click the ellipse at the top of the dark green spice shaker	To select them.
Press ⬚SHIFT⬚ and click the ellipse at the top of the right spice shaker	
8 In the Tools panel, select the Eyedropper tool	
9 Point to the ellipse at the top of the left spice shaker and click once	The ellipse with the dotted line.
10 Deselect the ellipse shapes	(Use the Selection tool.) To view the results.
11 Update and close the document	

Make sure students select the Selection tool before they try to deselect the ellipse shapes. Otherwise, they could accidentally change the color.

Unit summary: Applying basic color

Topic A   In this topic, you **adjusted the fill and stroke colors** for shapes. You applied color using the **Swatches panel** and the **Color panel**, and you **stored custom colors** in the Swatches panel.

Topic B   In this topic, you **set basic stroke formatting** for shapes. You **applied stroke color** to shapes, and you **adjusted the thickness of a stroke**. You also **created a dashed stroke**.

Topic C   In this topic, you used the **Eyedropper tool** to quickly sample fill and stroke attributes and apply them to other shapes.

Independent practice activity

In this activity, you'll apply fill and stroke colors to shapes. You'll also create a custom color and store it in the Swatches panel. You'll also format stroke attributes for a shape, and use the Eyedropper tool to quickly apply the same formatting attributes to other shapes.

1   Open the Recipe background color_practice document (located in the current unit folder.) Save the document as My recipe background color_practice.

2   Apply the Jade swatch to the fill of the three large clover shapes in the middle of the illustration. (*Hint*: Select the three shapes, then select the Fill icon in the Color panel, if necessary. Click on the Jade swatch in the Swatches panel.)

3   Use the Color panel to adjust the color for the middle clover shape so that it is slightly darker green. (*Hint*: Select the middle clover shape and drag the K slider in the color panel slightly to the right.)

4   Store the new darker green color in the Swatches panel. Title the color Dark Jade. (*Hint*: With the color selected, click the New Swatch button in the Swatches panel.)

5   Remove the stroke formatting from the three large clover shapes. (*Hint:* Select all three large clover shapes and click the Stroke icon in the Color panel. In the Swatches panel, click the [None] icon.)

6   Apply the Jade swatch to the fill of the grouped small clover shapes at the bottom of the illustration.

7   Apply a 4 pt stroke to the small clover shapes, and format it with the Dark Jade swatch. (*Hint*: With the small clover shapes selected, click the Stroke icon in the Color panel. Click the Dark Jade swatch in the Swatches panel. In the Stroke panel, choose 4 pt from the Weight list.)

8   Use the Eyedropper tool to apply the same fill and stroke formatting to the two large lighter green clover shapes. (*Hint*: Select the two large light green clover shapes on the right and the left of the dark green shape. Use the Eyedropper tool to click one of the smaller clover shapes.)

9   Deselect the shapes, then update and close the document.

Review questions

1 To apply color to the fill of an object by using the Color panel, you should:

A Select the item you want to apply color to, select the Stroke icon, and select the color.

B Select the color, select the Fill icon, and then select the item you want to apply color to.

c Select the item you want to apply color to, select the Fill icon, and select the color.

D Select the Fill icon, select the color, and then select the item you want to apply color to.

2 Which are ways you can apply a color to the stroke of a selected object? (Choose all that apply.)

A In the Color panel, click the Stroke icon, and then set the color you want by using the color sliders.

B Right-click the stroke of the object, and then select the color you want from the Swatches pop-up panel.

c In the Control panel, click the Stroke icon, and then select the color you want from the Swatches drop-down panel.

D In the Tools panel, click the Stroke icon, and select the color you want using either the Color or Swatches panels.

3 True or false? A swatch can be a color, gradient, or pattern.

True

4 You have a thick stroke applied to a shape, and you want the stroke to appear along the outside of the path of the shape. You should:

A Double-click the shape, and then choose the Align Stroke to Outside option and click OK.

B Click the Projecting cap button in the Stroke panel.

C Double-click the shape, and then choose the Projecting cap option and click OK.

D Click the Align Stroke to Outside button in the Stroke panel.

5 Which option is not available under Align Stroke in the Stroke panel?

A Align Stroke to Inside

B Offset Stroke

C Align Stroke to Outside

D Align Stroke to Center

6 The cap options for a stroke adjust the:

   A Appearance of corner anchor points that join two segments.

   B Appearance of the ends of open paths.

   C Thickness of the stroke.

   D Alignment of the stroke to the path.

7 True or false? When creating a dashed stroke, the dashes and gaps between them must be the same length.

False

8 To copy attributes by using the Eyedropper tool (Choose all that apply):

   A Select the item to which you want to apply the attributes, then use the Eyedropper tool to click the item whose attributes you want to copy.

   B Select the item whose attributes you want to copy, then use the Eyedropper tool to click on the item to which you want to apply the attributes.

   C Drag from the item whose attributes you want to copy to the item to which you want to apply the attributes.

   D Click the item whose attributes you want to copy, then Alt-click the items to which you want to apply the attributes.

9 True or false? The Eyedropper tool always applies both the fill and stroke attributes to the item it changes.

False

Unit 4

Drawing paths

Unit time: 65 minutes

Complete this unit, and you'll know how to:

A Import a raster image into a document by using the Place command.

B Draw complex shapes and paths by using the Pencil, Smooth, and Pen tools, and adjust paths by manipulating direction handles.

C Select and edit anchor points, join paths by using the Average and Join commands, and cut paths by using the Scissors tool.

Topic A: Raster images

Explanation

Designers often use raster images in their drawings, either as part of the illustration or to use them as templates when creating vector shapes and paths. If you include raster images, you can choose whether to link or embed them.

When you link a raster image, a preview of the image appears in drawing, but the actual image is not stored as part of the document. The *linked image* acts as a placeholder that refers the computer to the original file for printing or Web output. Because the original graphic isn't stored in the document, the linked preview isn't editable.

Embedded images are stored directly within the Illustrator document. Depending on the image file type, you can edit them with filters, and you do not have to worry about maintaining image links when sending the document to a printer. The only downside to embedded image files is that they add to the document's file size.

Embed raster images

To embed a raster image:

1 Choose File, Place to open the Place dialog box.

2 Navigate to the location of the image and select the image. If you don't see the name of the file you want, the file is in a format that Illustrator cannot read.

3 Verify that Link is cleared. (If you wanted to link the image, you would need to check Link.)

4 Click Place to embed the image.

Raster file types

The following list contains some common raster formats you can embed or link in Illustrator documents:

- Photoshop
- EPS
- TIFF
- JPEG
- BMP
- PCX
- CGM
- GIF89a
- PNG
- Targa
- Pixar
- Amiga
- IFF

Locking items

You can lock an image (or any other item in Illustrator) so that it cannot be moved or edited. This is useful if you are using an image as a template to create vector paths and shapes, since you can use the drawing tools to trace the image without accidentally moving it. To lock an item, verify it is selected and choose Object, Lock, Selection. To unlock items, choose Object, Unlock All.

Do it!   **A-1: Importing a raster image**

Here's how	Here's why
1 Choose **File, New...**	To open the New Document dialog box.
Name the file **Label elements**	
2 Verify that the document uses the Print preset, is 8.5 x 11, uses inches as the unit of measurement, and uses the landscape orientation	
Click **OK**	
3 Save the document in the current unit folder by using the name you specified	(Choose File, Save as, then verify that the current unit folder is visible, and click Save.) You'll import several raster images so that you can trace certain portions of them.
4 Choose **File, Place...**	To open the Place dialog box.
In the current unit folder, select the **Collage** image	You want to embed the image in the document, and not link it.
5 Near the lower-left corner of the dialog box, clear **Link**	If necessary.
Click **Place**	To import the image.
6 Reposition the image near the top-left corner of the artboard	
7 From the current unit folder, import the **Background** image	Choose File, Place, select Background, and click Place.
8 Reposition the image near the bottom-left corner of the artboard	Because you'll be using the drawing tools on top of the images, you'll lock them to keep from accidentally selecting or moving them.
9 Select both images	Click the first image. Press Shift and click the second image.
Choose **Object, Lock, Selection**	To lock both images in place.
10 Update the document	Choose File, Save.

Topic B: Basic drawing

This topic covers the following ACE exam objective for Illustrator CS3.

#	Objective
2.1	Given a tool, create an object. (Tools include: Pen, shape tools, and Pathfinder.)

Explanation

You previously created closed shapes by using the shape tools. You can create paths and shapes using the drawing tools, which include the Line Segment, Pencil, and Pen tools. You use the drawing tools to create straight and curved paths, which can be open or closed. An *open path* is a series of straight or curved lines in which the start and end points do not meet. A *closed path* is a series of straight or curved lines in which the start and end points meet, making it a closed shape.

Paths

A *path* consists of one or more connected lines. The connected lines are referred to as *segments*. The beginning and end of each segment in a path is marked by anchor points, which work like pins holding a wire in place.

You change the shape of a path by editing its anchor points. You control curves by dragging the direction points at the end of the direction lines that extend out from the anchor points, as shown in Exhibit 4-1. For an open path, the starting and ending anchor points for the path are called endpoints. To reshape a path by dragging its anchor points and direction points, you must use the Direct Selection tool. The Selection tool can select and move only the entire path.

There are two types of anchor points, corner points and smooth points. At a *corner point*, the path abruptly changes its direction. At a *smooth point*, path segments remain connected as a continuous curve. A corner point can connect straight or curving segments, but a smooth point always connects curving segments.

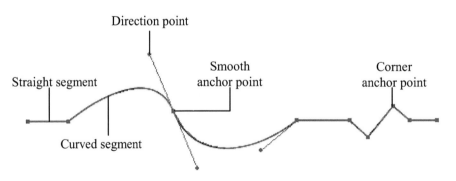

Exhibit 4-1: The components of a path

The Pencil tool

The simplest way to create paths is by using the Pencil tool. The Pencil tool mimics the way you would use a pencil and paper to draw. As you drag the pointer around the artboard, a path is created that follows the path of the pointer. In this way, the Pencil tool creates paths that appear "hand-drawn." When drawing with the Pencil tool, the anchor points of the path are added automatically. The following table describes methods for using the Pencil tool.

Method	Description
Create an open path	With the Pencil tool selected, position the pointer where you want the path to begin. Drag to create the path. Release the mouse button where you want the path to end.
Create a closed path	Using the Pencil tool, drag to begin creating a path. As you return to the point where you started, press Alt. The pointer changes to the shape of a pencil with a dark-colored eraser and a small loop near the point of the pencil. Point to the starting point of the path, and release the mouse button before releasing Alt. The end point joins with the start point of the path automatically.
Reshape a path	Verify that the path you want to reshape is selected and use the Pencil tool to redraw directly over the selected path to reshape it. To connect a new path to an existing path, press and hold Ctrl and drag from the new path to the end point of another path. Both paths must be selected in order to connect them.

The Smooth and Path Eraser tools

You might want to make a jagged path look smoother, or you might want to erase part of a path entirely. To do this, use the Smooth and Erase tools, which are located in the Pencil tool flyout menu. The following table describes the tools and how to use them.

Icon	Tool	Description
	Smooth tool	Smoothes paths and shapes. To smooth a path, select the Smooth tool and drag over the area of a selected path that you want to look smoother. This tool works on any path, no matter what tool was used to create the path.
	Path Eraser tool	Erases paths and anchor points from paths and shapes. To erase part of a path, select the Path Eraser tool and drag over the area of a selected path that you want to erase.

B-1: Using the Pencil and Smooth tools

Here's how	Here's why
Students must be able to see the entire pepper, including the entire stem.	
1 Zoom in on the collage image at the top of the artboard	(Select the Zoom tool and drag over the collage image to zoom in.)
	You'll draw a pepper shape, similar to the pepper in the image.
2 In the Tools panel, click	(The Pencil tool.) Before you begin drawing, you'll remove the fill attribute.
3 At the bottom of the Tools panel, click the Fill icon	(If necessary.) To make it active.
Click the None icon	
	(If necessary.) To remove any fill color.
Set the stroke to black	If necessary.
4 Point near the top-left side of the pepper, as shown	
	The pointer shows a pencil icon with a small "x" next to it. The x icon indicates that dragging will create a new path.

Tell students not to worry if they aren't able to trace the exact shape of the pepper.

Slowly begin to drag down (counterclockwise) around the outside of the pepper	
When you reach the bottom of the pepper, release the mouse button	A path appears from where you started to where you released the mouse button.
5 Point to the endpoint of the path	The pointer shows only a pencil icon, without the small "x."

Let students know if they make a mistake, they can drag over the line again to make corrections.

Continue dragging around the outside of the pepper, including the stem	

6 As you return to the starting point, press ⟨ALT⟩

The pointer shows a pencil icon with a small "o" shape next to it. Pressing Alt ensures that the path's two endpoints will meet, creating a closed path.

While pressing ⟨ALT⟩, release the mouse button

To complete the shape.

7 Zoom out to view the entire artboard

Press Ctrl+0.

Let students know they'll need to select the path to move the shape.

8 Use the Selection tool to drag the shape to a blank area of the artboard

You'll now edit the shape to make it appear smoother.

9 Zoom in on the pepper shape

Select the Zoom tool and drag over the pepper shape to zoom in.

10 In the Tools panel, hold down on the Pencil tool and select the Smooth tool

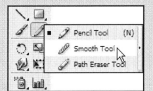

⚠ Make sure students have the pepper shape selected. The Smooth tool won't work if the shape is not selected.

11 Drag the pointer over any area of the shape that you want to make smoother

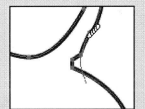

12 When the pepper shape is smooth enough, zoom out and update the document

The Pen tool

Explanation

ACE objective 2.1

The Pen tool is the most precise and flexible of the drawing tools. With it you can create very smooth-looking curves and straight segments to create paths of any shape.

When using the Pen tool, you specify the points that define the path. This is the opposite of the Pencil tool, with which you create the path and Illustrator automatically generates the points. When you use the Pen tool to create a curved path, you must specify the curved segments by manipulating the direction points extending from the anchor points, as shown in the previous Exhibit 4-1. The angle and distance that you drag the direction points control the intensity and direction of the curve.

To draw a path with straight segments:

1 With the Pen tool, point where you want the path to start.

2 Click to create an anchor point.

3 Point where you want the first segment to end; then click to place a second anchor point.

4 To continue adding segments to the path, point where you want the next segment to end, and click to add another anchor point. If you want to constrain the segments to 45° angles, press Shift as you click to create an anchor point.

5 To complete a path, press Ctrl to temporarily select the Selection tool, and click a blank area of the artboard to deselect the path. You can also complete a path by selecting a different tool in the Tools panel or by clicking the Pen tool in the Tools panel.

To draw a path with curved segments:

1 With the Pen tool, point where you want the path to start.

2 Press and hold the mouse button and drag in the direction you want the first segment to curve. (Because the direction point's angle controls the curve of the segment, you should drag the direction point in the direction you want the curve to go.)

3 Release the mouse button. The first segment won't appear until you add the second anchor point.

4 Point where you want the first curved segment to end; then press and hold the mouse button and drag to add the anchor point with direction points attached to it. Two direction points are added, one affecting the first segment's curvature, and the other affecting the next segment, if you add another segment.

5 Release the mouse button.

6 To continue adding segments to the path, point where you want the next segment to end, then drag or click to create the anchor point. If you want to constrain the direction points to 45° angles, hold down Shift as you drag.

7 To complete the path, press Ctrl and click a blank area of the artboard or select a different tool in the Tools panel.

Creating closed shapes

If you want to create a closed shape by using the Pen tool, use either of the techniques mentioned above to create the shape that you want. To close the path, point to the first anchor point on the path and click once. When you point to the first anchor point, the pointer changes to show the Pen icon with a small "o" next to it (🖉), indicating that clicking will close the path.

Drawing tool hotspots

Sometimes it's difficult to know where a drawing tool's hotspot is located. The *hotspot* is the part of the mouse pointer from which paths are drawn. For example, the Pen tool's hotspot is located at the tip of the Pen tool mouse pointer, so when you click or drag using the Pen tool, an anchor point is added at the position of the Pen tool mouse pointer's tip. To make it easier to locate a tool's hotspot, you can press Caps Lock so that the tool appears as a crosshair, with the hotspot located at the center of the crosshair. You can also view the rulers, which display a line indicating the location of the tool's hotspot, making it easier to identify where a point will be placed when you click with the Pen tool.

B-2: Using the Pen tool

Here's how	Here's why
1 Zoom in on the Background image near the bottom of the artboard	(Select the Zoom tool and drag over the Background image to zoom in.)
	You'll recreate some of the lines in the Background image to use in a spice label illustration.
ACE objective 2.1 2 In the Tools panel, click [🖋]	(The Pen tool.) To make the paths easier to see, you'll set them to be thicker.
3 In the Stroke panel, from the Weight list, select **3 pt**	(You'll need to expand the Stroke panel.) You'll begin by tracing one of the lines containing all straight segments at the top of the image.
4 Point to the beginning of one of the straight lines near the top-left corner of the image, and click once	To place an anchor point.
5 Point to the end of the first segment, and click again	
	To create a second anchor point and the first line segment.
6 Point to the end of the next diagonal line segment and click again	
	To create the second line segment.
7 Continue creating segments until you reach the end of the line	
Remind students that pressing Ctrl temporarily selects the Selection tool. 8 Press (CTRL) and click a blank area of the artboard	To deselect the line.
	Now you'll trace the arc shape near the lower-right corner of the image.
9 Point to the beginning of the arc near the lower-right corner of the image and click once, as shown	
	To create a new anchor point.

10 Point to the top of the arc

Press and hold the mouse button   To begin creating a curved segment.
and slowly drag to the right

When the curve closely matches
the curve of the arc, release the
mouse button

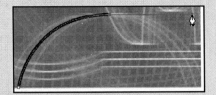

11 Point to the end of the arc, and
click once

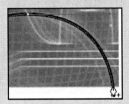

To complete the path.

12 Deselect the path   Press Ctrl and click a blank area of the artboard.

13 Update the document

Create complex paths

Explanation

You can use the Pen tool to create paths that include both curved and straight segments. To create complex paths, either click or drag to define each anchor point in the path. When you click with the Pen tool, you add an anchor point with no associated direction points. When you drag, you add an anchor point with direction points. If the two anchor points at either end of a segment were added by clicking, then the segment would be straight. If either one of the anchor points includes a direction point, the segment will be curved.

Do it!

B-3: Creating complex paths

Here's how	Here's why
1 Choose **View**, **Show Rulers**	(Or press Ctrl+R.) To view the rulers. Now you'll trace one of the lines that has both straight and curved lines.
ACE objective 2.1 2 Point to the beginning of the straight line near the middle-left side of the artboard as shown, and click once	 To create an anchor point.
3 Press (SHIFT), point to the end of the first segment, and click again	 To create a second anchor point, and the first line segment. (Pressing Shift creates straight segments that are restricted to 45° angles.)
4 Point to the middle of the curved segment of the path and drag down and to the right, as shown	 To begin creating the curve.
When the shape of the segment closely resembles the curve of the lines, release the mouse button	

5 Point to the end of the curved
   lines and click once

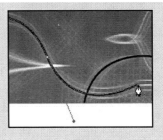

To create the second curve.

6 Press (*SHIFT*), point to the end of
   the line, and click once

To create the last straight segment.

7 Deselect the path

Press Ctrl and click on a blank area of the
artboard.

Adjust direction handles while drawing complex paths

By default, anchor points you create by dragging are created as smooth points, in which the path curves in the same direction as it passes through the anchor point. When you drag to add an anchor point, two direction points are added—one for each segment connected to the anchor point. The two direction points are attached to one another so they move together, maintaining the smooth point. However, you can create an anchor point as a corner point, in which the path's curvature changes direction as it passes through an anchor point, as shown in Exhibit 4-2.

To create a curving corner point as you draw a path, drag to create a smooth point, then press Alt and manipulate the direction handles the way you want them. Pressing Alt temporarily accesses the Convert Anchor Point tool, which you can use to drag direction points independently of one another, breaking their connection to one another.

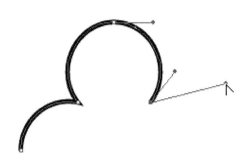

Exhibit 4-2: An example of adjusting the direction handles for an anchor point

B-4:   Adjusting direction handles while drawing complex paths

Here's how	Here's why

1 Point to the beginning of the set of lines at the left edge of the image

   Press ⟨ SHIFT ⟩ and drag to the right approximately **1** inch

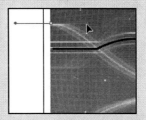

(Release the mouse button and the shift key.) To create a smooth point.

2 Point where the lines end in a sharp corner

   Drag to the right as shown, and don't release the mouse button

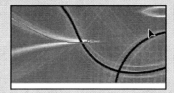

To begin creating the first curved line segment.

3 When the curve is similar to the curve of the lines, press ⟨ ALT ⟩, and slowly drag the right direction point back to the anchor point

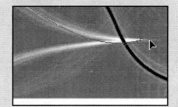

(Don't release the mouse button.) As you drag holding Alt, the direction handle on the opposite side of the anchor point remains in place.

   When the direction point is on the anchor point, release the mouse button and ⟨ ALT ⟩

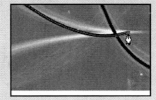

4 Point to the end of the lines that curve down and to the left, and drag down and to the left

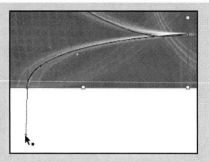

To create the second curved line segment.

5 Deselect the path

You'll create one last path by using the complex looking shape on the right side of the image.

6 Point to the top of the complex set of lines on the right side of the image, as shown

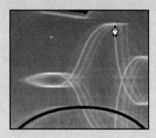

Press (SHIFT) and drag to the left approximately **.5** inches

To create a smooth point.

Demonstrate this step for students.

7 Point to the end of the first curved segment; then drag up and to the left

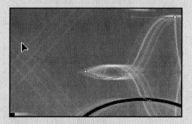

(Don't release the mouse button.) To create the first curve.

Press (ALT) and drag the left direction point back to the right and up so that it mirrors the opposite direction point, as shown

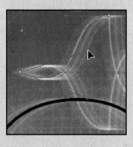

Release (ALT) and the mouse button

To set the corner point.

8 Point to the bottom of the next curved segment and drag to the right

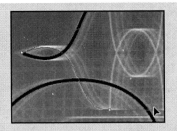

(Don't release the mouse button.) To begin creating the next curve.

When the curve matches the curve of the line in the image, press and hold (ALT), and drag the direction point straight up as shown

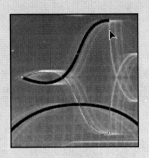

To set the corner point.

9 Press (SHIFT) and point to the end of the next curve

While holding (SHIFT), drag straight down

To create the curved segment.

10 Deselect the path, and update the document

(Press Ctrl and click a blank area of the artboard.) You'll work more with this path later.

Topic C: Select and edit paths

This topic covers the following ACE exam objectives for Illustrator CS3.

#	Objective
2.1	Given a tool, create an object. (Tools include: Pen, shape tools, and Pathfinder.)
2.2	Given a scenario, choose the appropriate tool to select an object or the points of an object. (Scenarios or tools include: Selection tool, Direct Selection tool, Isolation mode, Select menu commands.)

List the contents of your document

Explanation

You'll often need to edit anchor points and direction handles after you've completed a path or closed shape. This could include dragging anchor points to a new location, adjusting direction handles, or even adding new anchor points or deleting anchor points. In addition, you might want to join two or more existing paths into one path, or cut one path into two.

Editing anchor points

ACE objective 2.2

To edit anchor points in an existing path, use the Direct Selection tool in combination with the Add Anchor Point, Delete Anchor Point, and Convert Anchor Point tools located in the Pen tool flyout menu. The following list describes ways you can edit anchor points:

- To move an anchor point, select it by using the Direct Selection tool and drag the anchor point to a new location.

- To adjust the curvature of a curved segment, use the Direct Selection tool to click the segment or its anchor point so the associated direction points appear, and drag a direction point to adjust the curvature.

- To add anchor points to a path, select the Add Anchor Point tool (from the Pen tool flyout menu) and click anywhere on a path to add a new anchor point.

- To delete anchor points from a path, select the Delete Anchor Point tool, and click any existing anchor point on a path to delete it. When you delete an anchor point, the two segments on either side of the anchor point become one segment.

- To remove the direction points associated with an anchor point, select the Convert Anchor Point tool, and click the anchor point. You can also drag from an anchor point to create a smooth point, or drag the direction points directly to create a corner point.

Selecting path components with the Direct Selection tool

ACE objective 2.2

You can use the Direct Selection tool to move an anchor point, a direction point, or an entire path. You can't select individual anchor points or direction points by using the Selection tool. You can use the Direct Selection tool to select anchor points and direction points individually only when the entire path is not already selected.

A path displays the following characteristics to indicate which of its components are selected:

- When all anchor points are selected, they all appear solid, and no direction points appear. When all anchor points are selected, you have to deselect the path before you can select individual anchor points or direction points.
- Anchor points appear hollow to indicate they're not selected, but that some component of the path is selected, as shown in Exhibit 4-3.
- Direction points appear for individually selected anchor points or segments.

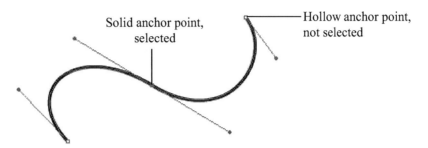

Solid anchor point, selected

Hollow anchor point, not selected

Exhibit 4-3: A path with an individual anchor point selected

The part of the path you click determines which path component is selected. Use these Direct Selection tool techniques to select path components:

- Click the fill within a shape to select the entire path, just as though you'd clicked it with the Selection tool. To select individual anchor or direction points, you'll have to first deselect the path.
- Click an anchor point to select it individually and display all direction handles associated with the segments on either side of the anchor point.
- Drag across one or more anchor points to select them without selecting anchor points outside the area you drag across.
- Click a segment to display its associated direction points, if any.
- Press Shift and click multiple anchor points on a path to select them.

Do it!

C-1:   Editing anchor points

ACE objective 2.1
ACE objective 2.2

Here's how	Here's why
1 Use the Selection tool to select the top path consisting of straight segments	You'll adjust the path so that it contains curves instead of straight line segments, similar to the other lines.
2 In the Tools panel, from the Pen tool flyout menu, select the Delete Anchor Point tool	Pen Tool (P) Add Anchor Point Tool (+) Delete Anchor Point Tool (-) Convert Anchor Point Tool (Shift+C) You'll start by deleting a couple of unnecessary anchor points.

3	Point to the second anchor point from the left in the path and click once	To delete the anchor point.

4	Observe the selected line	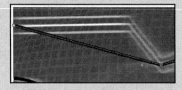

The anchor point is removed and the straight line segment connects the remaining points.

5	Click the next anchor point	To delete the point, and create a long straight segment.

6	Click on the third anchor point from the left	To create the following path. You'll now reposition some of the points.

7	Select the Selection tool	

8	Point to the second anchor point and drag the anchor point to the left	The entire path moves, because you can't manipulate individual anchor points by using the Selection tool. You'll undo this step and use the Direct Selection tool.

9	Press CTRL + Z	To undo moving the path.

10	Click in a blank part of the artboard	To deselect the path. When all anchor points are selected, you have to deselect the path before you can use the Direct Selection tool to manipulate individual points.

ACE objective 2.2

11	Select the Direct Selection tool	So you can select individual anchor points instead of the entire path.

12	Point to any segment of the path and click	To select the path without selecting all of the anchor points.

13	Point to the second anchor point and drag the anchor point to the left, as shown	The anchor point you dragged is solid, indicating that it is selected.

The other anchor points are hollow, indicating that they're not individually selected.

14 Drag the third anchor point slightly to the left, as shown

You'll now convert some of the points to smooth points.

ACE objective 2.1

15 In the Tools panel, from the Delete Anchor Point tool flyout menu, select the Convert Anchor Point tool

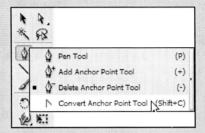

16 Click the third anchor point in the path and hold

(Don't release the mouse button.)

Drag slowly to the right, as shown

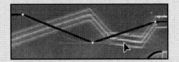

To add direction points to the anchor point, creating curvature for the segments on each side of the anchor point.

17 Drag the second anchor point down and to the right

To convert the point to a smooth point.

Drag the fourth anchor point up and to the right

To complete the shape of the path.

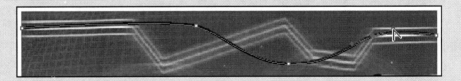

18 Update the document

Joining paths by using the Average and Join commands

Explanation

You might want to connect two or more paths together to create one path or to create a closed shape. To do this, you need to use the Average and Join commands in the Object, Paths submenu.

Average command

The Average command moves two or more anchor points to a position that is the average of their current positions. For example, if you select two path endpoints, the Average command calculates the distance between them, and then positions them one on top of the other midway between their current locations.

To use the Average command, select the anchor points you want to average by using the Direct Selection tool; then choose Object, Path, Average to open the Average dialog box, shown in Exhibit 4-4. You can select to average the anchor points along the horizontal (x) axis only, the vertical (y) axis only, or both axes.

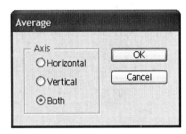

Exhibit 4-4: The Average dialog box

Join command

The Join command connects the endpoints of an open path to create a closed path, or joins the endpoints of two open paths so they become a single path. To use the Join command, you must select only the endpoints, and not the entire paths you want to connect. To join two paths (or create a closed shape), select the endpoints by using the Direct Selection tool and choose Object, Path, Join. If the endpoints are a distance from each other, a straight segment is created automatically, connecting the two endpoints. If the anchor points are already overlapping, then they're combined as a single anchor point.

Path options in the Control panel

You can reference some path commands in the Control panel. For example, you can activate the Join command by clicking the Connect selected endpoints button, as shown in Exhibit 4-5. You can also use path command buttons to convert corner points to smooth points or vice versa, and to show or hide handles for anchor points. The buttons are visible when you are using either the Direct Selection tool or the Pen tool.

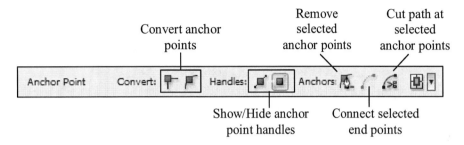

Exhibit 4-5: Path options in the Control panel

C-2: Joining paths with the Average and Join commands

Here's how	Here's why
1 Select the Selection tool	You'll use the partially completed complex path on the right side of the image to create a closed shape. You'll duplicate the path, rotate it, and connect the two paths.
2 Drag the complex path on the right side of the image to a blank area of the artboard	
3 Duplicate the path	Press Alt and drag the path to create a duplicate.
4 Rotate the duplicated path 180°	Point just above the top-right handle of the bounding box, press Shift, and drag to rotate the image 180°.
5 Position the duplicated shape as shown	 You'll join the two paths to make a closed shape.
6 Using the Zoom tool, drag to zoom in where the open ends of the two paths overlap at the top of the shape, as shown	
7 Select the Direct Selection tool	To join the two paths, you need to select both endpoints.
8 Drag to select the overlapping endpoints, as shown	 You'll average the two points so that they overlap each other exactly.

9 Choose **Object**, **Path**, **Average...**	To open the Average dialog box.
Verify that **Both** is selected, and click **OK**	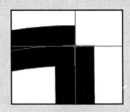
	The two points are positioned together. You'll now join the two paths.
10 In the Control panel, click 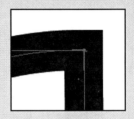	(The Connect selected end points button.) The Join dialog box appears.
Verify that **Corner** is selected, and click **OK**	
	Two of the curve handles disappear, and the paths are joined with a single anchor point in place of the two overlapping anchor points.
11 View the entire artboard	(Press Ctrl+0.) You'll now join the two remaining open endpoints to make a closed shape.
12 Using the Zoom tool, zoom in on the two remaining open anchor points, as shown	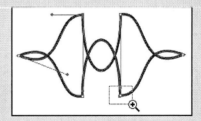
13 Select the two open endpoints	Using the Direct Selection tool, drag across the two endpoints.
14 Average the two anchor points	Choose Object, Path, Average.
15 Join the two anchor points	(Click the Connect selected end points button in the Control panel.) To close the path.
16 View the entire artboard, and update the document	

Cutting paths using the Scissors and Knife tools

Explanation You might want to separate one path into two paths. You can do this by using either the Scissors tool or the Knife tool.

The Scissors tool

The Scissors tool cuts paths at precise locations that you specify. To cut a path, select the Scissors tool, and point to the part of the selected path that you want to cut. If you are cutting a closed shape, and you want to remove a portion of the shape, click at the start and end points for the part of the path that you want to remove, as shown in Exhibit 4-6. You can click anywhere on a path to cut it, even in the middle of a segment where no anchor points currently exist.

Using the Scissors tool, click on two locations on a path to cut a section from the path

The resulting cut segment

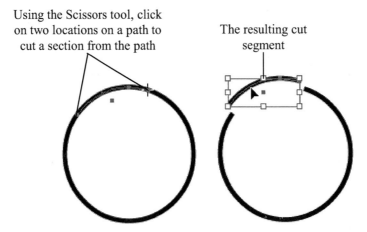

Exhibit 4-6: An example of using the Scissors tool to cut a shape

The Knife tool

The Knife tool splits paths in a fashion similar to the Scissors tool, but it affects paths a little differently. To cut a shape by using the Knife tool, select the Knife tool and drag across the shape. The Knife tool works only on closed shapes or paths with fills applied, and the resulting paths are always closed shapes. For example, if you use the Knife tool to drag across the middle of a rectangle, the rectangle is cut into two smaller closed shapes, as shown in Exhibit 4-7.

Using the Knife tool, drag across a closed shape to cut it.

The original shape is converted into two closed shapes.

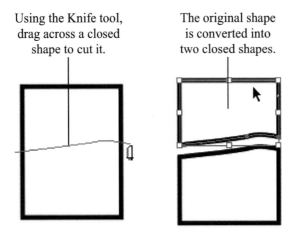

Exhibit 4-7: An example of cutting a shape using the Knife tool

C-3: Cutting paths using the Scissors tool

Here's how	Here's why
1 Zoom in on the Background image	(Near the bottom of the artboard.) You'll cut one of the paths so that it becomes two paths, and then reposition the paths across the background.

Here's how	Here's why
2 Using the Selection tool, select the path in the lower-left corner, as shown	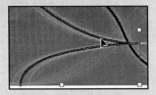 The path with the sharp corner point.
3 In the Tools panel, from the Eraser tool flyout menu, select the Scissors tool	
4 Point to the corner point and click once	 To cut the path.
5 Select the Direct Selection tool	
6 Point to the right-most anchor point of the selected path and drag up and to the right, as shown	

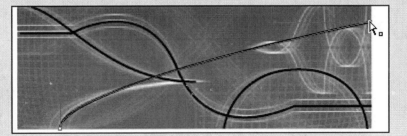

7 Press ⟨SHIFT⟩ and drag the anchor   To adjust the shape of the curved segment.
   point handle on the left-most
   anchor point up, as shown

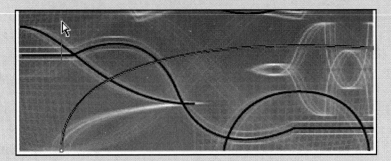

8 Click the unselected portion of the   To select it.
   cut path

9 Drag the left-most anchor point up
   approximately .5 inches

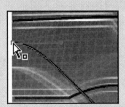

10 Drag the right-most anchor point
    to the opposite side of the
    background, as shown

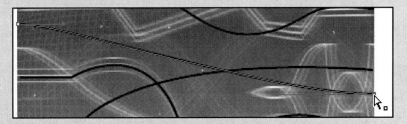

11 Using the direction handles,
    reshape the path as shown

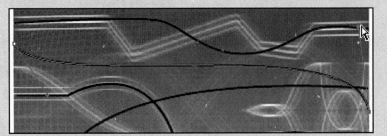

12 Deselect the path

13 View the entire artboard

14 Update and close the document

Unit summary: Drawing paths

Topic A   In this topic, you learned how to **link or embed raster graphics** in an Illustrator document.

Topic B   In this topic, you learned how to **draw shapes and paths by using the basic drawing tools**. You created freeform shapes using the **Pencil tool**, and you created more precise paths by using the **Pen tool**.

Topic C   In this topic, you learned how to **select and edit paths**. This included **manipulating anchor points by using the Add Anchor Point, Delete Anchor Point**, and **Convert Anchor point tools**, as well as cutting paths by using the **Scissor and Knife tools**. Lastly, you joined open paths by using the **Average and Join commands**.

Independent practice activity

In this activity, you'll draw paths and shapes using the Pencil and Pen tools. You'll also manipulate anchor points using the Delete Anchor Point, Add Anchor Point, and Convert Anchor Point tools.

1 Open the Drawing_practice document (located in the current unit folder). Save the document as My drawing_practice.

2 Using the Pencil tool, trace the large sliced mushroom near the bottom of the image. (*Hint*: Select the Pencil tool and drag around the outside of the sliced mushroom. When you return to the starting point, press Alt to complete the shape.)

3 Using the Smooth tool, smooth any portions of the path that seem jagged. (*Hint*: Select the Smooth tool, and drag over the areas of the path you want to smooth.)

4 Switch to the Pen tool, and trace the outline of the bay leaf near the upper-right corner of the image. (*Hint*: Click where you want to create corner points, and drag where you want to create smooth points.)

5 Using the Delete Anchor Point, Add Anchor Point, or Convert Anchor Point tools, adjust the shape of the bay leaf, if necessary.

6 Update and close the document.

Review questions

1 True or false? When you place a raster image in an Illustrator document, it is always contained within the file, adding to the file size.

   False. (You can choose to link to the original image file.)

2 To prevent an item from being moved or edited, you can _____ it.

   lock

3 With which tool do you directly specify where points appear along the path as you create it?

   A Pencil

   B Pen

   C Smooth

   D Any of the above

4 Dragging with the Pen tool:

   A Creates an anchor point and extends a direction point to affect the adjoining segment's curvature.

   B Creates multiple anchor points.

   C Creates a corner point to make a sharp change in the path's direction between the adjoining segments.

   D Moves the anchor point you drag.

5 True or false? You can move one anchor point on a path independently by dragging it with the Selection tool.

   False

6 Which can the Convert Anchor Point tool do? (Choose all that apply.)

   A Delete an anchor point.

   B Remove direction points associated with an anchor point.

   C Add direction points to an anchor point that had none, creating a smooth point.

   D Drag a direction point associated with a smooth point to change it to a corner point.

Unit 5

Working with text

Unit time: 50 minutes

Complete this unit, and you'll know how to:

A Add text to an illustration by using the Type tool, and import text by creating a type container and using the Place command.

B Convert shapes to type containers, format a type container, position type on a path, and convert text to outlines by using the appropriate text tools and commands.

Topic A: Add text

This topic covers the following ACE exam objectives for Illustrator CS3.

#	Objective
4.2	Add type to a document.
4.3	Manage the composition of text by using panels, menus, and preferences settings.

Type tools

Explanation

Logos, advertisements, and other graphics are designed to communicate, and text is often an important part of that communication. You can add and modify text using any of the six text tools: Type, Area Type, Type on a Path, Vertical Type, Vertical Area Type, and Vertical Type on a Path. You can use these tools to add text horizontally or vertically, define type containers, or add text along curved or straight paths.

The Type and Vertical Type tools

The Type and Vertical Type tools are used to insert text horizontally or vertically in an illustration. You can also use these tools to define rectangular boxes called *type containers*, which act as holding areas for text.

ACE objective 4.2

To insert text horizontally or vertically:

1 Select the Type tool or Vertical Type tool. The shape of pointer changes to an I-beam bordered by a dotted rectangle. If you select the Vertical Type tool, the I-beam appears horizontally.

2 Click in the artboard to create an insertion point for the text. The insertion point appears in the form of a small, blinking vertical line. When you type using the Vertical Type tool, the insertion point appears horizontally.

3 Type the text you want to add to the illustration. If you are using the Vertical Type tool, the characters appear one below the other.

4 To deselect the text, select the Selection tool and click anywhere in the artboard.

If you select existing text with the Selection tool, a blue horizontal line appears below the typed text (or through the middle of the characters if you are using the Vertical Type tool). This is the baseline of the text and defines the direction in which the text flows. Also, a bounding box appears around the text, which you can use to reposition, rotate, or resize the text.

The Character panel

ACE objective 4.3

After typing text, you'll likely need to format it by changing its size, font, style, or leading. To apply these changes, you use the Character panel (shown in Exhibit 5-1), which you can view by choosing Window, Type, Character.

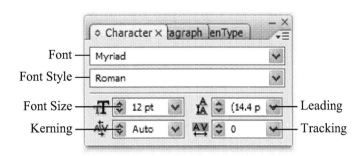

Exhibit 5-1: The Character panel

To change the font family, size, and style of text, select the text and select the options you want from the Character panel's Font, Font Style, and Font Size lists. You can also enter a size value in the Font Size box.

To adjust character spacing, you can specify values in the Tracking and Kerning boxes. Tracking varies the spacing between all the characters in the selected text. Kerning varies the spacing between two or more selected characters. If the text you enter includes multiple lines, you can adjust the distance between the baselines of the lines of text by specifying a value in the Leading box.

You can also expand the panel to display additional options for text. The full panel includes options for underlining, strikethrough, and the language (for use with spelling checks).

The Paragraph panel

ACE objective 4.3

To format paragraphs of text, you can use the options available in the Paragraph panel, shown in Exhibit 5-2. To view the Paragraph panel, choose Window, Type, Paragraph.

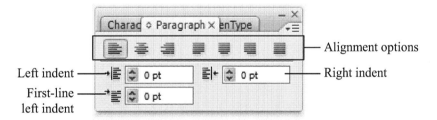

Exhibit 5-2: The Paragraph panel

The following table describes some of the paragraph formatting options.

Icon	Option	Description
	Align left	Aligns text to the left of a text block. By default, all text is left-aligned.
	Align center	Aligns text to the center of a text block.
	Align right	Aligns text to the right of a text block.
	Justify with last line aligned left	Justifies lines so they extend from the text block's left edge to its right edge, and aligns the last line of text to the left, without fully extending it to the right.
	Justify with last line aligned center	Justifies lines, and aligns the last line of text to the center of a text block.
	Justify with last line aligned right	Justifies lines, and aligns the last line of text to the right of a text block.
	Justify all lines	Justifies all lines, including the last line.
	Left indent	Controls the distance between the left edges of the baseline of text and the left wall of a type container. A positive indent value shifts the baseline inward, and a negative value shifts the baseline toward the outside.
	Right indent	Controls the distance between the right edges of the baselines of text and the right wall of a type container.
	First-line left indent	Controls the left indent of only the first line of a paragraph. You can assign it a negative value to make the text appear as a hanging indented text block, with the first line protruding to the left.

Type formatting using the Control panel

ACE objective 4.3

To save screen space, you can also access type formatting options in the Control panel. The options are visible each time you select text in a drawing. You can set the font, font style, and size for text by using the boxes in the Control panel, or you can view the entire Character and Paragraph drop-down panels by clicking the blue "Character" or "Paragraph" links, as shown in Exhibit 5-3.

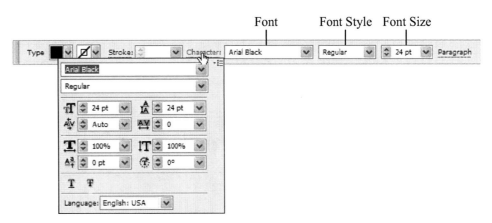

Exhibit 5-3: The Character drop-down panel in the Control panel

Change text color

You can change the color of text by using the same methods you would use when applying color to shapes. Select the text and specify the colors you want in the Fill and Stroke boxes in the Tools panel or the Color panel.

Select text

The following list describes some efficient ways to select text by using the Type or Vertical Type tools.

- To select individual characters, point to the beginning of the characters you want to select, and drag to select them.
- To select a word, double-click anywhere on the word you want to select.
- To select an entire paragraph, triple-click anywhere in the paragraph you want to select.

Do it!

A-1:   Creating text

Here's how	Here's why
1 Open **Shaker label_text**	Located in the current unit folder.
Save the document as **My shaker label_text**	(In the current unit folder.) You'll add some text to the spice shaker label.
2 In the Tools panel, click T	The Type tool.
3 Click a blank area of the artboard	To place the insertion point.
Type **Outlander Spices**	
4 Select the Selection tool	A bounding box appears around the text.
5 Center the text on the gold rectangle in the middle of the label	
	You'll format the text so that it's more prominent.
6 Select the Text tool, then triple-click the text	To select it.
7 In the Control panel, from the Font list, select **Times New Roman**	
8 From the Font Size list, select **18 pt**	You'll increase the type size by 1 pt.
9 Click the up arrow on the left side of the Font Size box	To increase the type size to 19 pt.
10 Using the Selection tool, reposition the text in the center of the gold rectangle	You'll make the text white.
11 In the Control panel, click the Fill icon	
	To expand the Swatches drop-down panel.
In the drop-down panel, click the **White** swatch	
12 Click a blank area of the artboard	To deselect the text. You'll also add some text to indicate which label you are working with.

ACE objective 4.2

ACE objective 4.3

Let students know they can use the arrow keys to nudge the text into position.

13 Place a new insertion point on a blank area of the artboard	In the Tools panel, select the Type tool and click on a blank area of the artboard.
Type **Parsley Flakes**	
14 Center the text in the large white rectangle	
	(Select the Selection tool and drag the text.) Near the bottom of the label.
15 Select the Text tool, then triple-click the text	To select it.
16 Set the font for the text as **Arial Black**	In the Control panel, from the Font list, select Arial Black
17 Set the size of the text to **24** pt	From the Font Size list, select 24. The text is now too large, and overlaps the edge of the rectangle.
18 Select the Type tool	
19 Click just to the left of the letter **F** in the word **Flakes**	To place the insertion point.
Press (← BACKSPACE)	To delete the space.
Press (SHIFT) + (↵ ENTER)	To create a line break instead of a paragraph break, so the second word moves to a new line but remains in the paragraph for formatting purposes.

ACE objective 4.3

20 In the Control panel, click the Paragraph link	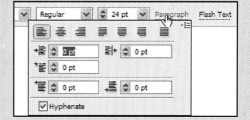
	To expand the Paragraph drop-down panel.
In the drop-down panel, click	(The Align center button.) To center the type.

21 Reposition the text in the center of the rectangle

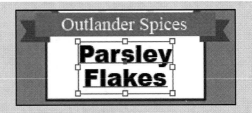

(Use the Selection tool and the arrow keys to position the text.)

You'll adjust the leading for the text so the two words are closer together.

22 Select the Selection tool

If necessary.

23 In the Control panel, click the Character link

To expand the Character drop-down panel.

24 From the Leading list, select **24**

The space between "Parsley" and "Flakes" is reduced.

Click a blank area of the artboard

To close the drop-down panel.

25 Update the document

Import text

Explanation

You can add text to an illustration from an external file, such as a Microsoft Word document. Illustrator supports the following formats for importing text:

- Microsoft Word 97, 98, 2000, 2002, 2003, and 2007
- Microsoft Word for Mac OS X and 2004
- RTF (Rich Text Format)
- Plain text (ASCII) with ANSI, Unicode, Shift JIS, GB2312, Chinese Big 5, and Cyrillic encoding

Imported text retains its character and paragraph formatting. For example, text from a Microsoft Word document will have the same font and style formatting once you import it into an Illustrator drawing. You can also set encoding and formatting options when importing text from a plain text file.

ACE objective 4.2

To import text from an external file:

1 Choose File, Place to open the Place dialog box.
2 Navigate to the location of the file, select the file, and click Place.
3 If you are importing text from a plain text (.txt) file, do the following, and then click OK:
    - If necessary, change the encoding information for the file. Illustrator usually determines this information automatically.
    - If you want to remove extra paragraph returns, check Remove at End of Every Line, or Remove Between Paragraphs.
    - If you want to replace extra spaces with a tab character, set the number of spaces in the Extra Spaces box.
4 If you are importing text from a Microsoft Word (.doc) or Rich Text Format (.rtf) file, do the following, and then click OK:
    - If you want to include table of contents text, footnotes/endnotes, or index text, check those options.
    - If you do not want to import the existing formatting of the text, check Remove Text Formatting.

Type containers

When you import text from an external file, if no insertion point is placed in the document, Illustrator flows the text so it fits within the artboard's printable area. However, you might want to add the placed text to only a specific portion of the artboard. In that case, you should create a type container for the text before you import it.

To create a type container, select the Type tool and drag to create a rectangular box. When you release the mouse button, a blinking insertion point appears inside the type container's upper-left corner, marking where the imported text will begin. When the imported text reaches the right edge of the type container, it automatically flows to the next line. If the imported text can't all fit in the container, a red + (plus) sign appears in the lower-right corner of the box, similar to the example in Exhibit 5-4. To view all the text, you can increase the size of the type container by dragging a corner, just as you would resize a shape.

If you have specific questions about any of our products, their uses, or any of their contents, please call our spice hotline at 800-555-SPCS, and we'll be glad to assist

Exhibit 5-4: An example of a type container with more text than it can display

Do it!

A-2: Importing text

ACE objective 4.2

Here's how	Here's why
1 Select the Type tool	You'll import some text providing information about the spice hotline number.
2 Point near the top-left corner of the label	
Drag down and to the right, as shown	
	To create a type container.
3 Choose **File, Place...**	To open the Place dialog box.
4 Navigate to the current unit folder and select the **Hotline** Word document	
Click **Place**	To open the Microsoft Word Options dialog box. You'll keep the formatting applied to the text in Microsoft Word.

5 Verify that **Remove Text Formatting** is cleared

   Click **OK**   To import the text. You'll verify that the formatting is how you want it.

6 Using the Type tool, select **www.outlander.com** in the text   In the text, click to the left of the text and then drag to make the selection.

7 In the Control panel, verify that the formatting is Arial Black, 12 pt

8 In the Control panel, click the blue Character link   To view the Character drop-down panel.

9 In the Leading box, verify the leading is **18** pt

10 Click [T]   (The Underline button.) To underline the text.

11 Resize the type container

(If necessary.) (Select the Selection tool and drag the type container handles.) So that all the text is visible.

12 Deselect the text and update the document

Topic B: Alter text

This topic covers the following ACE exam objective for Illustrator CS3.

#	Objective
4.5	Create outlines of type by using the Create Outlines command.

Creative type

Explanation

In addition to basic type formatting, you can also manipulate text in creative ways. You can insert type inside custom shapes, flow type along paths, and convert type to paths that you can reshape just as you'd reshape other Illustrator paths.

Type area tools

Earlier, you learned to insert text at a point as well as inside a rectangular type container. You can also add type inside any closed shape by using the Area Type and Vertical Area Type tools. The Area Type tool converts shapes into type containers in which text flows horizontally. The Vertical Area Type tool converts shapes into type containers in which text flows vertically from the upper-right corner downward to the left corner.

To convert shapes into type containers:

1   Draw a closed shape by using either the shape tools or the drawing tools.
2   Select the Area Type tool or the Vertical Area Type tool. The pointer appears as an I-beam surrounded by two curved lines. If you select the Vertical Area Type tool, the pointer is horizontal.
3   Click anywhere on the path of the shape. The path loses all its paint attributes and changes into a type container. If you are using the Area Type tool, the insertion point appears as a vertical blinking line near the top-left corner. If you are using the Vertical Area Type tool, the insertion point appears as a horizontal blinking line near the top-right corner.
4   Import or type the text you want.

Format type containers

After you've added text to a type container, you can add color to the container or change its shape. To do so, first select the path of the container by using the Direct Selection tool. When you do, the handles for the type container change to anchor points, which you can use to reshape the container. When you change the shape of the container, the text automatically shifts inside the modified closed path. Also, any fill or stroke attributes you apply will affect the container instead of the text inside the container. In addition, you can also use the Area Type Options dialog box to format a type container.

To resize a container by using the Area Type Options dialog box:

1   Using the Selection tool, click the text in the type container to select it.
2   Choose Type, Area Type Options to open the Area Type Options dialog box, shown in Exhibit 5-5.
3   Specify the settings you want, and click OK.

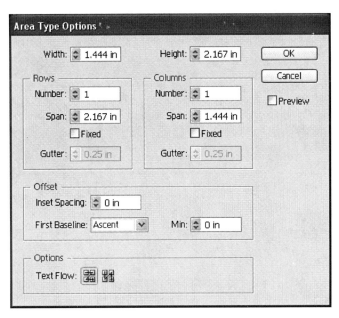

Exhibit 5-5: The Area Type Options dialog box

The following table describes the options in the Area Type Options dialog box.

Option	Description
Width and Height	Sets the width and height of the type bounding box.
Rows and Columns	Sets the number of rows or columns for the bounding box. The Span field specifies the row height or column width. The Gutter field specifies the space between the rows or columns. The Fixed check box determines what will happen if the bounding box is resized. If the Fixed check box is checked, then the row height or column width remains fixed, and the number of rows or columns will change.
Inset Spacing	Sets a margin inside the bounding box.
First Baseline	Determines where the first line of text in the bounding box falls. You can make the first line stick up above the bounding box, or fall a specific distance below the top of the bounding box.
Text Flow	Determines how the text flows between the columns and rows of text.

Do it!

B-1: Using the Area Type tool

Here's how	Here's why
1 Select the Ellipse tool	You'll add some text that flows within the boundaries of an ellipse.

Let students know the fill and stroke attributes are irrelevant, since they'll be converting the ellipse to a type container.

Here's how	Here's why
2 On the right side of the label, create an ellipse, as shown	
3 From the Text tool flyout menu, select the Area Type tool	

Let students know they need to click the ellipse path, and not inside the ellipse.

Here's how	Here's why
4 Point to the ellipse path and click once	The formatting attributes for the ellipse are removed, and a blinking insertion point appears at the top of the ellipse.
5 Import the **Parsley Flakes** Word document	(Choose File, Place, navigate to the current unit folder, select Parsley Flakes, and click Place. In the Microsoft Word Options dialog box, verify that Remove Text Formatting is cleared, and click OK.)
	You want the boundary of the ellipse to be visible, so you'll inset the text.
6 Choose **Type**, **Area Type Options...**	To open the Area Type Options dialog box.
7 In the Offset section, to the left of the Inset Spacing box, click the up arrow once	

8 Check **Preview**

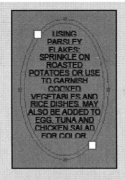

To view the results.

Click **OK**   To close the dialog box.

9 Resize the ellipse   (If necessary.) So that all of the text is visible. You'll format the ellipse so that it is white with a black border.

10 Press ⟨CTRL⟩ and click a blank area of the artboard

To deselect the text.

To format the ellipse type container, you need to select just the container.

11 Choose **View, Outline**   To see all the paths in the illustration.

12 Select the Direct Selection tool

13 Click the path of the ellipse

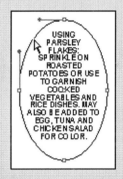

To select just the ellipse.

14 Choose **View, Preview**   To view the illustration with color again.

15 In the Tools panel, verify that Fill is selected

16 In the Swatches panel, click the White swatch

(You'll need to expand the Swatches panel.) To make the ellipse white. You'll also add a black stroke to the ellipse.

17 In the Tools panel, click the Stroke icon

To make the stroke attribute active. Also, the Color panel expands.

18 In the Color panel, click the Black swatch

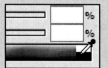

In the Stroke panel, from the Stroke Weight list, select **2 pt**

You'll need to expand the Stroke panel.

19 Deselect the ellipse, and update the document

Position type on a path

Explanation

You can position text to follow the shape of path. To do this, you use the Type on a Path tool or the Vertical Type on a Path tool to convert the path into the baseline for the text. You can type text perpendicular or parallel to the path, or make it appear above or below the path. You can position type along either open or closed paths.

To convert a path into the baseline of text and position text along it:

1   Using the drawing tools or the shape tools, draw either an open or closed path.

2   Select the Type on a Path tool or the Vertical Type on a Path tool. The pointer changes to a vertical I-beam with a curved line cutting through it. If you select the Vertical Type on a Path tool, the I-beam is horizontal.

3   Click the path at the point where you want the text to start. All the paint attributes of the path are removed, and the insertion point appears on the path as a blinking line.

4   Add the text you want. The text flows along the path. If you use the Vertical Type on a Path tool, the characters appear stacked.

Modify text paths

You might want to reposition text on the path. To move the text, click the text by using the Selection tool. A bounding box appears around the path, and three blue brackets appear—at the beginning of the type, at the end of the path, and at the midpoint between the start and end brackets. Point to one of the blue brackets, and drag it along the path, as shown in Exhibit 5-6.

You can reshape the path by using the Direct Selection tool to select it and modifying its anchor points or segments. The text automatically arranges itself along the new modified path.

Exhibit 5-6: An example of repositioning text on a path

The Type on a Path Options dialog box

If you want to format type on a path, you can use the Type on a Path Options dialog box. You can apply effects, such as Rainbow, Skew, or 3D Ribbon to the text, or you can change how the text is aligned to the path.

To apply effects and align text to a path:

1   Using the Selection tool, click the text to select it.

2   Choose Type, Type on a Path, Type on a Path Options to open the Type on a Path Options dialog box, shown in Exhibit 5-7.

3   From the Effect, Align to Path, and Spacing lists, select the appropriate options, and click OK. The value in the Spacing box determines the distance between the characters of the selected text. You can also check the Preview box to see the changes applied to the selected text.

4   Click OK.

Exhibit 5-7: The Type on a Path Options dialog box

Do it!   **B-2: Positioning type on a path**

Here's how	Here's why
1 Zoom in on the large ellipse in the center of the label	
2 Select the Selection tool	
3 Click on the gold border of the ellipse	To select it. You'll create a second ellipse that is slightly smaller than the existing one. You'll use the center point of the existing ellipse to position the new one.
4 Select the Ellipse tool	
5 Point to the center point of the selected ellipse	The small blue square represents the center of the selected ellipse.
Press ⌐ALT⌐ and drag up and to the right	(Don't release the mouse button.) To begin creating an ellipse from the center outward.
6 Create an ellipse that is smaller than the existing ellipse, as shown	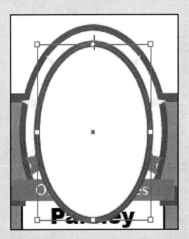 You'll use the ellipse to position some text.
7 From the Area Type tool flyout menu, select the Type on a Path tool	
8 Point to the top-left path of the new ellipse and click once	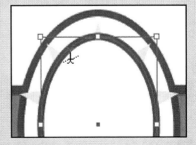 The ellipse loses its formatting, and an insertion point appears. Before you add the text, you'll set the text formatting you want.

Let students know they need to click the path of the ellipse, and not inside the ellipse.

9	In the Control panel, from the Font list, select **Arial**	If necessary.
	From the Font Size list, select **12 pt**	If necessary.
10	Expand the Character drop-down panel, and click **T**	(The Underline button.) To deselect it.
11	Expand the Paragraph drop-down panel, and click the Align Left button	
12	Type **Quality Spices Since 1989!**	You'll position the text so that it is centered at the top of the ellipse.
13	Select the Selection tool	
14	Choose **View, Hide Bounding Box**	(Or press Shift+Ctrl+B.) To make it easier to see the brackets on the text path.

⚠ *Make sure students move the left bracket.*

15	Point to the left-most end bracket, as shown	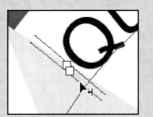
		You'll move the end bracket, and then use the middle bracket to move the text on the ellipse.
	Drag to the right and position the bracket just past the end of the text, as shown	
		To place the end bracket at the end of the text.

16	Point to the middle bracket, as shown		
	Drag to the left		
			To center the text on the top of the ellipse.
17	Choose **View**, **Show Bounding Box**		(Or press Shift+Ctrl+B.) To make the bounding box visible again.
18	Resize the ellipse so that the text flows just inside the original ellipse, as shown		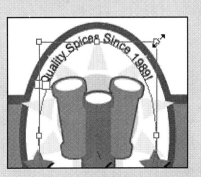
			(If necessary.) Press Shift+Alt and drag the top-right boundary box resize handle.
19	Deselect the text and view the entire artboard		Press Ctrl+0.
	Update the document		

If time allows, you might want to let students experiment with the effects available in the Type on a Path Options dialog box. Have them revert back to the basic settings when they're done.

Convert type to outlines

Explanation

ACE objective 4.5

You can redesign the look of type by reshaping the characters. For example, you might have a large headline in which you want to modify one or more of the characters to make them more unique looking. To do this, you need to convert the type to outlines by using the Create Outlines command in the Type menu. Creating outlines converts the characters in the selected type into closed shapes that you can modify. Once you've converted type to outlines, you cannot edit the text or adjust the font.

Do it!

B-3: Converting text to outlines

Here's how	Here's why
1 Select the Type tool	(You might have to select the tool from the Type on a Path tool flyout menu.)
	You'll add the word "Outlander" so that it stretches across the width of the label.
2 Click a blank area of the artboard	To place the insertion point.
Type **Outlander**	
3 Triple-click the text to select it, then set the font to Arial Black	Choose Arial Black from the Font list in the Control panel.
4 Set the font size to 72 pt	(Choose 72 pt from the Font Size list.)
	You'll customize the first letter "O" to make it more creative.
5 Select the Selection tool	
6 Choose **Type, Create Outlines**	To convert the text to outlines.
7 Select the Direct Selection tool	
8 Click a blank part of the artboard	To deselect the text.
9 Click inside the first letter **O**	
	To select it.
10 Press and hold CTRL	To view the bounding box for the shape. (Pressing Ctrl temporarily selects the Selection tool.)
Rotate the **O** to the left, as shown	
	You'll also create an extension from the top-left corner of the letter.
Release CTRL	To hide the bounding box.

ACE objective 4.5 (beside step 6)

Make sure students click inside the "O" to select it and not one of the paths. (beside step 9)

11 Press (SHIFT) and click on the top-left anchor point, as shown

To deselect it.

Release (SHIFT) and click the deselected point

To select the point, and deselect the other points.

12 Drag the anchor point to the left, as shown

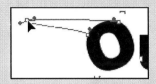

To create an extension.

13 Using the Selection tool, select the other letters in **Outlander**

(Click one of the other letters.)

You'll position and format the word in the label.

14 Position the text along the bottom of the label, as shown

15 Select the Eyedropper tool, and click the green background of the label

To color the text with the green color.

16 In the Colors panel, verify that **Fill** is selected

Drag the K color slider to **15**

17 Press (CTRL) + (SHIFT) + (I)

To send the text to the back of the stacking order.

Press (CTRL) + (I)

To bring the text one step forward in the stacking order. (It should now be in front of the green background.)

18 Deselect the text

To view the results.

19 Update and close the document.

Unit summary: Working with text

Topic A   In this topic, you learned to use the **Type and Vertical Type tools** to add text to an illustration. You also learned how to **import text** from an external document and format text by using the **Character and Paragraph panels**.

Topic B   In this topic, you learned to creatively alter text. You **inserted text into custom shapes, positioned text on a path**, and **converted type to outlines**.

Independent practice activity

In this activity, you'll manually add text to a document, as well as import text within a type container. You'll also create type along a path.

1 Open the Chicken recipe text_practice document (located in the current unit folder). Save the document as My chicken recipe text_practice.

2 Add the text **Chicken Stuffed with Spices** just below the image of the plate of chicken, similar to the example in Exhibit 5-8. Format the text as 24 pt, Arial Black. Apply the Jade swatch to the text.

3 Create a type container in the open space to the left of the "Directions" text. (*Hint*: Using the Type tool, drag to create the container.) Import the Ingredients_practice Word document into the container (located in the current unit folder), similar to the example in Exhibit 5-9. (*Hint*: Choose File, Place.) Keep the same formatting applied to the text in the Word document.

4 Readjust and reposition the type container, if necessary, so that all of the text is visible. (*Hint*: Drag the handles of the container to resize it.)

5 Add the text **Outlander Spices** so that it follows the curve at the top of the plate of chicken image, similar to the example in Exhibit 5-10. (*Hint*: Create a circle that is slightly larger than the plate of chicken. Use the Type on a Path tool to add the text.) Format the text as 26 pt, Arial. Apply the Jade swatch to the text.

6 Update and close the document.

Exhibit 5-8: The recipe after step 3 of the activity

Exhibit 5-9: The recipe after step 4 in the activity

Exhibit 5-10: The recipe after step 6 in the activity

Review questions

1 True or false? When you click a document with the Type tool, text you create will automatically wrap to multiple lines within the artboard.

   False

2 Which are ways to change the font for a selected portion of text? (Choose all that apply.)

   A In the Control panel, choose a font from the Font list.

   B In the Paragraph panel, choose a font from the Font list.

   C In the Open Type panel, choose a font from the Font list.

   D In the Character panel, choose a font from the Font list.

3 How can you underline a portion of selected text? (Choose all that apply.)

   A In the Control panel, expand the Character drop-down panel, and then click the Underline button.

   B Choose Type, Smart Punctuation to open the Smart Punctuation dialog box, then check Underline and click OK.

   C In the Character panel, choose Show Options from the panel menu to expand the panel, and then click the Underline button.

   D Choose Type, Change Case, Underline.

4 Which are ways you can select portions of text? (Choose all that apply.)

   A Point to the beginning of the characters you want to select and drag to select them.

   B Double-click anywhere on a word to select the entire word.

   C Triple-click anywhere in a paragraph to select the paragraph.

   D Place the insertion point anywhere in a type container; then choose Edit, Select All to select all the text in the container.

5 The Type on a Path tool creates:

   A Type that flows within a shape such as an ellipse.

   B Type characters with editable outlines you can distort.

   C Vertical type.

   D Type with a baseline that conforms to a path.

6 Which are ways to create a type container? (Choose all that apply.)

   A Using the Type tool, drag on the artboard.

   B Using the Area Type tool, drag on the artboard.

   C Using the Type tool, click inside a shape to convert it to a type container.

   D Using the Type tool, click on the edge of a shape to convert it to a type container.

7 You have a portion of selected text that you want to convert to outlines. You should:

   A Choose Type, Create Outlines.

   B In the Character panel, choose Show Options from the panel menu to expand the panel, and then click the Create Outlines button.

   C Using the Selection tool, double-click the text; then check Create Outlines and click OK.

   D In the Paragraph panel, choose Show Options from the panel menu to expand the panel, and then click the Create Outlines button.

Unit 6

Layers

Unit time: 40 minutes

Complete this unit, and you'll know how to:

A Create new layers, change layer stacking order, and hide and lock layers by using options in the Layers panel.

B Organize layer content and duplicate layers by using the Layers panel.

Topic A: Layers

Explanation

When you create a complex illustration, it can become difficult to select individual items from among many. In addition, it can be difficult to stack overlapping items in the correct order. To address these problems, you can organize items into layers. A layer combines items and groups into a single unit in the Layers panel that can be hidden, locked, displayed as outlines, moved up and down in the stacking order, and whose items can be selected and manipulated all at once. You can even create sublayers within a layer to further organize its contents. By layering items, you can reduce the complexity of an illustration by breaking it down into manageable components.

The Layers panel

Each Illustrator document has at least one layer by default (titled "Layer 1"), and each item you create in an illustration is automatically added to that layer unless you specify otherwise.

For complex illustrations, you can use the Layers panel to create new layers and assign items to them. If you select a layer, and create a new item, the item will automatically be assigned to the selected layer.

Each item assigned to a particular layer is indented below the layer in the Layers panel, as shown in Exhibit 6-1. For example, if a layer contains a rectangle and a circle, you can see those items listed in the Layers panel by clicking the small triangle to the left of the layer name, which expands the layer. Illustrator titles each layer item based on the type of item it is (such as <Path> or <Group>). In the Layers panel, you can expand a group to display each item in the group.

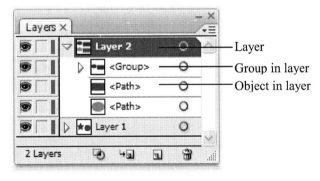

Exhibit 6-1: The Layers panel

Along the bottom of the Layers panel are four buttons you can use to create new layers or sublayers, delete layers, or make or release clipping masks. (A *clipping mask* is a vector path that frames other objects so that those objects are visible only within the clipping mask.)

The following table describes the buttons.

Button	Name	Description
	Make/Release Clipping Mask	If you want to create a clipping mask, you can use this button to create or release the clipping mask. Both items you want to use for the mask must be on the same layer.
	Create New Sublayer	Creates a new sublayer below the current selected top-level layer.
	Create New Layer	Creates a new top-level layer above the current selected top-level layer.
	Delete Selection	Deletes the selected layer, sublayer, or item listing in the Layers panel, along with any corresponding items in the illustration.

Create layers

To create a new layer:

1 Press Alt and click the Create New Layer button in the Layers panel. The Layer Options dialog box appears, as shown in Exhibit 6-2. (You can also click the Create New Layer button to create a new layer, and then double-click the layer to open the Layer Options dialog box.)

2 In the Name box, enter a unique name for the layer.

3 Set the options you want for the layer by editing the layer color or selecting from the available check boxes.

4 Click OK to create the layer.

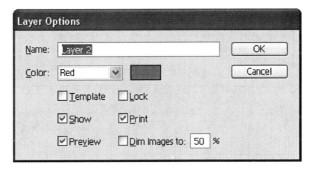

Exhibit 6-2: The Layer Options dialog box

The following table explains the options in the Layer Options dialog box.

Item	Description
Color	Sets the layer's color setting. Selected items in the layer will display the color in the bounding box and selection lines.
Template	Establishes the layer as a template layer. You can use template layers when you want to base a new illustration on an existing piece of artwork, such as when you want to trace an image.
Lock	Prevents changes to the artwork contained in the layer.
Show	Displays all the artwork contained in the layer. If this option is not checked, the artwork is hidden.
Print	Makes the artwork contained in the layer printable.
Preview	Displays the artwork contained in the layer in Preview view.
Dim Images	Reduces the intensity of linked images contained in the layer to a specified percentage. This is commonly used with template layers.

Create sublayers

You can also create sublayers within a layer by using the same technique, except instead of clicking the Create New Layer button, you click the Create New Sublayer button. The options you select in the Layer Options dialog box affect the sublayer, and not the top-level layer.

After creating the new layer or sublayer, select it to make it the current layer and then, in the artboard or scratch area, create the artwork that you want to place in the layer.

Moving items between layers

After you've created additional layers, you can reassign existing items to the new layers. To move items among layers:

- In the Layers panel, expand the layer containing the item you want to move, and drag the item to another layer in the Layers panel.
- When you select an item in an illustration, a selection icon appears to the right of the item in the Layers panel, as well as next to the layer containing the item, as shown in Exhibit 6-3. You can drag the selection icon up or down to another layer to move the selected item to that layer.

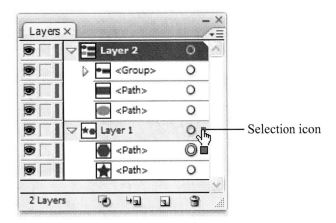

Exhibit 6-3: Reassigning items to a new layer by dragging the selection icon

Do it!

A-1: Creating a new layer

Here's how	Here's why
1 Open **Shaker label_layers**	Located in the current unit folder.
Save the document as **My shaker label_layers**	(In the current unit folder.) You'll use this label for many different spices. To do this, you will create layers for the text. You'll begin by moving the "Parsley Flakes" text to its own layer.
2 Expand the Layers panel	
3 In the panel, press ⎇ALT and click ▣	(The Create New Layer button.) To create a new layer and open the Layer Options dialog box. When you press Alt, the Layer Options dialog box opens. If you click the Create New Layer button without pressing Alt, the layer is added without the dialog box opening.
4 In the Name box, enter **Parsley text**	
Click **OK**	To close the dialog box. You'll also rename the original "Layer 1" layer.
5 In the Layers panel, double-click **Layer 1**	To open the Layer Options dialog box.
6 In the Name box, enter **Background**	
Click **OK**	You'll move the "Parsley Flakes" text from the Background layer to the Parsley text layer.
7 Using the Selection tool, select the text **Parsley Flakes**	
Press ⇧SHIFT and click the text within the ellipse	(Near the right side of the label.) To select both portions of parsley text.
8 In the Layers panel, point to the small blue square on the right side of the Background layer	
Drag the small blue square up to the Parsley text layer	The boundary boxes for the selected elements turn red, indicating they are now on the Parsley text layer.
9 Update the document	

Layer stacking order

Explanation

The top layer in the Layers panel is the front layer in the artwork window, which means that all its contents will appear in front of the contents of other layers where those contents overlap. Likewise, the bottom layer in the Layers panel is the back layer in the artwork window, so its contents will appear behind the contents of other layers where those contents overlap. You can rearrange the stacking order of layers, sublayers, or individual layer objects by dragging them up or down in the panel, as shown in Exhibit 6-4.

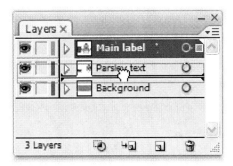

Exhibit 6-4: Rearranging the stacking order of a sublayer by dragging it

Create new layers in the stacking order

To some degree, you can also create new layers where you want them in the stacking order. By default, a new layer is positioned above a selected layer when you click the New Layer button. So to position a layer where you want it in the stacking order, select a layer, click the New Layer button, and the new layer is added above the layer you selected.

Do it!   ## A-2:   Changing layer stacking order

Here's how	Here's why
1 Create a new layer titled **Main label**	(In the Layers panel, press Alt and click the Create New Layer button. In the Name box, enter Main label and click OK.) You'll use the new layer to divide the unchanging text portions of the label, and some of the background elements.
2 Select all the objects on the artboard	Press Ctrl+A.
Press (SHIFT) and click the green background rectangle	To deselect it.
Press (SHIFT) and click the Parsley Flakes text	To deselect it. This includes the text "Parsley Flakes" as well as the text within the ellipse.
Press (SHIFT) and click the large outlined Outlander text	To deselect it as well.
3 In the Layers panel, drag the small blue square from the Background layer to the Main label layer	
4 Deselect the objects	(Click a blank area of the artboard.) By moving the selected elements to the new layer, the text "Parsley Flakes" is covered up. You'll change the stacking order of the layers to correct this.
5 In the Layers panel, drag the Main label layer down below the Parsley text layer	 The text "Parsley Flakes" is visible again.
6 Update the document	

Hide and lock layers

Explanation

When you edit items on one layer, you might want to lock or hide other layers. This prevents you from making unintentional changes to the contents of other layers.

Lock layers

When you lock a layer, you cannot add, move, change, or delete any item on that layer until you unlock it again. To lock a layer, click the lock box to the left of the layer name on the Layers panel, or open the Layer Options dialog box and check Lock. An icon in the shape of a lock appears in the edit column, as shown in Exhibit 6-5. To unlock a layer and make it editable, simply click the lock icon to the left of the layer name.

Hide layers

You can hide layers so that they are not visible, editable, or printable. To hide a layer, click the eye icon in the visibility box to the left of the layer row on the Layers panel. The eye icon disappears and so does the artwork of that layer from the artwork window. To show the hidden layer, click its visibility box to show the eye icon again.

You can also lock or hide all the other layers, except the selected layer by choosing Lock Others or Hide Others from the Layers panel menu.

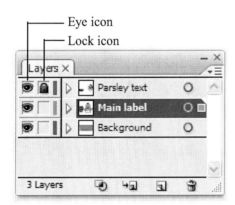

Exhibit 6-5: The Eye and Lock icons in the Layers panel

A-3: Hiding and locking layers

Here's how	Here's why
1 In the Layers panel, click in the second column to the left of the Main label layer, as shown	
	To lock the layer so that the elements that make up the main portion of the label cannot be selected.
2 Click the text at the top of the large ellipse	You cannot select the text.
Click one of the spice shakers	The background shapes are selected. When a layer is locked, you can still select elements that are behind the locked layer.
3 Deselect the items	You'll hide the Main label and Parsley text layers so that you can add some elements to the background of the label.
4 In the Layers panel, to the left of the Main Label layer, click the eye icon, as shown	
	To hide the layer.
5 Hide the Parsley text layer	(Click the Eye icon to the left of the Parsley text layer.)
	You'll add some curved lines from another document to make the background more interesting.
6 Open **Label elements_layers**	Located in the current unit folder.
7 Select and copy the grouped lines at the lower-left corner of the artboard.	(The curved lines that overlap the blue background image.) Press Ctrl+C to copy the lines.
8 Choose **Window, My shaker label_layers**	To return to the label illustration.

9 Paste and position the lines as shown

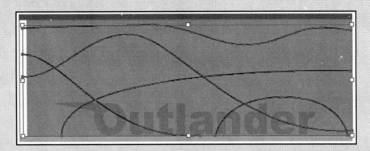

Press Ctrl+V to paste the lines. Resize the lines so that they stretch across the entire width of the label.

10 Select the Eyedropper tool and click the light green rectangle at the bottom of the background

To apply the light green color to the lines. The light green color is applied as a fill. You'll switch it so that the light green color is applied as a stroke.

11 In the Tools panel, click 🔁

The Swap Fill and Stroke icon.

12 In the Stroke panel, set the stroke weight to **4 pt**

13 Press ⌃CTRL + ⇧SHIFT + [

To send the lines to the back of the stacking order.

Press ⌃CTRL + [

To bring the lines one step forward in the stacking order. (They should now be in front of the green background.)

14 Deselect the lines

To view the results. (Be sure to select the Selection tool before clicking on a blank area of the artboard.)

15 Show the Parsley text and Main label layers

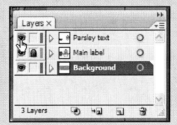

In the Layers panel, click in the left-most columns to the left of these layers so the eye icons appear.

16 Update the document

Topic B: Manipulate layers

Explanation

Generally, it's less confusing if you work with as few layers as possible in your illustrations. However, if you work with multiple layers, there are some things you can do to make working with them less confusing. This includes organizing and renaming layers and layer contents, duplicating layers, and deleting layers that are no longer necessary.

Organizing layer contents

It can be difficult to identify what each item listed within a layer represents in the illustration. By default, Illustrator identifies each path as <Path> in the Layers panel, and each group as <Group>. With many layer objects all named similarly, it becomes difficult to identify and manage them. For this reason, it's a good idea to give your layer objects more descriptive names.

Rename layer objects

You already learned how to name layers as you create them. To rename layer objects, you need to first decipher what each object represents. Even though each layer object includes a small thumbnail image, it might be difficult to identify the item. A quick way to view the item is to click in the Selection column to the right of the layer object, as shown in Exhibit 6-6. When you do, a small colored square is visible, and the item is selected in the illustration.

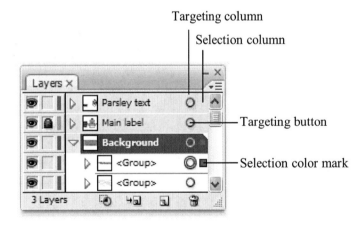

Exhibit 6-6: The targeting and selection options in the Layers panel

To rename a layer object, double-click the object listing in the Layers panel to open the Options dialog box, shown in Exhibit 6-7. The Options dialog box is similar to the New Layer dialog box, except you can only specify a name for the object and decide whether to lock it or change its visibility.

Exhibit 6-7: The Options dialog box for a layer object

Targeted layers

When you select items by using the Layers panel, it's important to understand the differences between the Targeting and Selection columns (shown in Exhibit 6-6). You can use the Targeting column to apply appearance attributes and effects to an entire layer. For example, if you click the Target icon next to a layer, and then apply a drop shadow effect, all items in the layer take on the drop shadow effect. However, if you move an object to another layer, that object will no longer have a drop shadow because the effect is attached to the layer, and not to the individual items. Similarly, if you add a new item to the targeted layer, it will automatically take on the drop shadow effect, and you will not be able to remove the effect unless you move the item to a different layer, or remove the effect entirely from the targeted layer. For this reason, make sure to click in the selection column whenever you want to select specific items in a layer.

Do it! **B-1: Organizing layer content**

Here's how	Here's why
1 In the Layers panel, click the triangle to the left of the Background layer	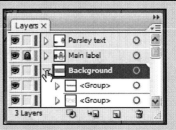
	To expand the layer.
Scroll to the bottom of the list of layer objects	(If necessary.) So that all the objects are listed.
2 To the right of the first <Group> object, click in the Selection column as shown	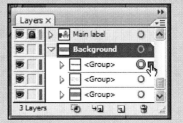
	The outlined text "Outlander" is selected on the artboard. You'll rename the group so that you can identify it easier in the Layers panel.
3 Double-click the first <Group> item	To open the Options dialog box.
4 In the Name box, enter **Outlander text**	
Click **OK**	You'll also rename the other two grouped items.
5 To the right of the second <Group> item, click in the Selection column	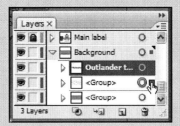
	The group of lines is selected on the artboard.
6 Rename the <Group> item as **Background lines**	Double-click the group listing to open the Options dialog box; then enter Outlander text in the Name box and click OK.
7 Rename the third <Group> item as **Label background**	

8	Click the triangle to the left of the Background layer	To hide the list of its contents.
9	Update the document	

Duplicate layers

Explanation

You might need to duplicate layers to create different versions, with minor changes in each version. For example, you might want to print the illustration in a second language. Instead of recreating the illustration, or saving it under a different name, you can duplicate the relevant layers and then show or hide them depending on what you want to print. When you duplicate a layer, the items on the layer are also duplicated.

To create a duplicate layer, select the layer you want to duplicate and choose Duplicate <Layer name> from the Layers panel menu. You can also duplicate a layer by dragging the layer to the Create New Layer button at the bottom of the panel, or by dragging the layer to a new location in the stacking order, and then pressing Alt as you release the mouse button.

Delete layers

To delete layers, select the layer you want to delete and click the Delete Selection button at the bottom of the panel. When you do, a dialog box appears asking if you're sure you want to delete the layer. Click OK to delete the layer. To bypass the dialog box, you can also drag the layer to the Delete Selection button. When you delete a layer, the items on the layer are deleted as well.

Do it!

B-2: Duplicating a layer

Here's how	Here's why
1 In the Layers panel, drag the Parsley text layer down to the Create New Layer button	
	You'll create duplicate layers of the Parsley text layer to hold the text for different types of spices.
Release the mouse button	
	To create a duplicate layer. A new layer titled "Parsley text copy" appears above the Parsley text layer.
2 Rename the layer as **Bay leaves text**	Double-click the layer, enter Bay leaves text in the Name box, and click OK.
3 Hide the Parsley text layer	Click the Eye icon to the left of the Parsley Text layer.

4 Use the Type tool to select the text **Parsley Flakes**

(Located on the artboard.) Select the Type tool and drag to select the text.

Type **Bay Leaves**

To replace the text. Add a soft paragraph return so that the text flows on two lines.

5 On the right side of the label, select the Using Parsley Flakes text

(The text within the ellipse.) Click to place the insertion point in the text; then press Ctrl+A.

6 Import the **Bay leaves** Word document

In the current unit folder. (Choose File, Place, select Bay leaves, and click Place. In the Microsoft Word Options dialog box, verify that Remove Text Formatting is cleared, and click OK.)

You can also let students switch between the Parsley text layer and the Bay leaves text layer to see the results.

7 Update and close all open documents

Unit summary: Layers

Topic A   In this topic, you learned to **create new layers** and **reassign items to them**. You also learned to **adjust the stacking order for layers**, and to **lock layers** and **adjust their visibility**.

Topic B   In this topic, you learned to **manipulate layers** by **renaming sublayers**, **duplicating layers**, and **deleting layers**.

Independent practice activity

In this activity, you'll create new layers for a document, and assign existing objects to them. You'll also duplicate layers and use them to update the information in an illustration.

1 Open the Chicken recipe_layers practice document (located in the current unit folder). Save the document as My chicken recipe_layers practice.

2 Create two new layers for the document. Label them "Chicken recipe" and "Logo." Rename the default Layer 1 as "Background." (*Hint*: Press Alt and click the Create New Layer button in the Layers panel to create the new layers. Double-click the Layer 1 layer to rename it.)

3 Select the logo in the upper-left corner of the recipe (the logo is the three spice shakers overlapping the sun shape) and reassign it to the Logo layer. (*Hint*: Select the logo and drag the selection marker in the Layers panel from the Background layer to the Logo layer.)

4 Select the text "Chicken Stuffed with Spices," the Ingredients text, and the Directions text and reassign them to the Chicken recipe layer.

5 Duplicate the Chicken recipe layer. (*Hint*: Drag the Recipe text layer down to the Create New Layer button.)

6 Rename the duplicate layer "Potatoes recipe" and hide the Chicken recipe layer. (*Hint*: Click the eye icon to hide the layer.)

7 On the Potatoes recipe layer, select the text "Chicken Stuffed with Spices" and replace it with "Princely Potatoes."

8 Replace the Ingredients text and the Directions text by using the Potatoes ingredients_practice and Potatoes directions_practice documents (located in the current unit folder).

9 Update and close the document.

Review questions

1 Which are true about layers? (Choose all that apply.)

   A You can hide a layer.

   B You can view a listing of all items within a layer by expanding the layer in the Layers panel.

   C When you lock a layer, you can select its items but not move them.

   D You can use the Layers panel to change the stacking order of both layers and the items within a layer.

2 To move an item from one layer to another (choose all that apply):

   A Drag its name between items in that layer.

   B Drag its name to the layer name.

   C Drag its selection icon to the layer name.

   D Drag the item from the artboard to the layer in the Layers panel.

3 True or false? You can create a sublayer within a layer.

   True

4 True or false? If you click a layer's targeting button and apply an effect, the effect applies to each item within the layer individually, and will continue to do so if you move the item to another layer.

   False

5 To duplicate a layer (choose all that apply):

   A Drag it to the Create New Layer button at the bottom of the Layers panel.

   B Ctrl-click its name.

   C Press Alt as you drag it to a new location in the stacking order.

   D Choose Duplicate <Layer name> from the Layers panel menu.

Unit 7

Working with fills and colors

Unit time: 40 minutes

Complete this unit, and you'll know how to:

A Import swatches from other documents, add swatches to the Swatches panel, and save a swatch library by using the Save Swatch Library command.

B Apply a gradient fill to a shape by using the Gradient panel, and adjust a gradient by using the Gradient tool and the Gradient panel.

C Adjust the opacity for a shape by using the Transparency panel.

Topic A: Swatch libraries

This topic covers the following ACE exam objective for Illustrator CS3.

#	Objective
3.1	Create spot colors and add them to the Swatches panel.

Managing swatches

Explanation

As you work with multiple illustrations, you'll want to use colors across documents. For example, if you're creating more than one illustration for a company, it's likely you'll want to use the same colors. To manage colors, you can import them from document to document and store them in swatch libraries.

Import swatches from other documents

The simplest way to access colors used in a previous illustration is to import them.

 To import a swatch library from another document:

1 In the Swatches panel, click the Swatch Libraries menu button. When you do, a list of libraries becomes visible. From the list, select Other Library to open the Select a library to open dialog box.

2 Navigate to the location of the document from which you want to import a swatch library.

3 Select the document and click Open. A new swatch panel appears. The name of the swatch panel is the same as the document you imported the Swatch library from, and it includes any custom colors created in that document. You can either work with the new swatch library, or drag the colors you want to the Swatches panel in the current document.

Do it!

A-1: Importing swatches from other documents

Here's how	Here's why
1 Open **Chicken recipe_colors**	Located in the current unit folder.
Save the document as **My chicken recipe_colors**	You'll import colors from the Spice shaker illustration to use in the recipe.
2 Open **Spice shaker illustration_colors**	Located in the current unit folder.
3 Expand the Swatches panel	
	(If necessary.) The panel includes a group of colors that you want to use in the recipe.
4 Choose **Window**, **My chicken recipe_colors**	To return to the recipe document.
5 In the Swatches panel, click [icon]	(The Swatch Libraries menu button.) To expand the list of swatch libraries.
From the list, select **Other Library...**	To open the Select a library to open dialog box.
6 Navigate to the current unit folder	
7 Select **Spice shaker illustration_colors**	
Click **Open**	
	A new swatch panel appears in the work area that shows the swatches used in the Spice shaker illustration_colors document. You'll add the color group to the current document's Swatches panel.
8 Point to the folder icon in the bottom row of the swatches	
Drag the folder to the current document's Swatches panel	To add the color group.

9	Close the Spice shaker illustration_colors swatch panel	
10	Drag the Swatches panel tab from the panel group to a blank area of the artboard	To undock it and convert it to a floating panel.
11	Using the Selection tool, click the large rectangle surrounding the recipe	To select it.
12	Apply the Dark Green swatch to the stroke of the rectangle	In the Tools panel, click the Stroke icon and click the Dark Green swatch in the Swatches panel.
13	Click one of the stars in the illustration near the upper-left corner of the recipe	
	Apply the Gold swatch to the fill of the stars	In the Tools panel, click the Fill icon and click the Gold swatch in the Swatches panel.
14	Update and close all open documents	

Opening existing swatch libraries

Explanation

Illustrator includes a variety of swatch libraries with harmonious colors such as those in the Beach or Victorian color panels, or third-party color systems such as PANTONE swatches. When you load a swatch library, it appears in a new panel. To open an additional swatch library, select the library you want from the Swatch Libraries menu list.

When a Swatch library is open, you can use it the same way you use the Swatches panel in the current document. To apply colors, simply click the swatches you want. You can also move swatches from the swatch library to the Swatches panel by either dragging them, or selecting the color you want to include and clicking the New Swatch button in the Swatches panel. If you are using only one or two colors, this can save you from having to keep the swatch library panel open.

Spot colors

ACE objective 3.1

Earlier, you used CMYK color to format items. However, printing CMYK colors can be very expensive because it requires four color plates to complete the job. As an alternative you can use spot colors, which is sometimes more cost effective.

A *spot color* is a color that is printed with a single pre-mixed ink. Spot colors are often used to replicate a color accurately and consistently, such as a color used in a company's logo. When you choose a color from a swatchbook that you know your printer has available and that matches the finish on your paper stock (coated or matte finish, for example), then you can be assured of an exact color match. Illustrator contains libraries of color matching systems, including PANTONE, TruMatch, FocolTone, and others. Spot colors are also useful when you want a specialty ink, such as those for shiny metallic colors. When printing three or fewer colors, spot colors are less expensive to print than process colors because fewer printing plates need to be made.

Convert spot color to process color

Although it is often convenient to choose spot colors from a swatch library, you must be careful to limit the number of inks. If you include color raster images in your illustrations, they would require four-color printing regardless of the colors you choose. If your illustration already requires four-color printing, you can keep spot colors from increasing the printing cost (because spot colors would require additional printing plates) by converting spot colors to process colors.

If you want to convert a spot color to a process color, you must first move the spot color swatch to the Swatches panel in the current document. To do this, select the spot color you want to use, and it will automatically appear in the current document's Swatches panel. Spot color swatches have a small black dot in the lower-right corner, as shown in Exhibit 7-1.

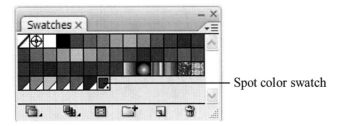

Exhibit 7-1: An example of a spot color swatch

To convert the spot color to a process color:

1   Double-click the spot color swatch to open the Swatch Options dialog box.
2   From the Color Mode list, select CMYK.
3   From the Color Type list, choose Process Color as shown in Exhibit 7-2.
4   Click OK to close the dialog box and convert the color.

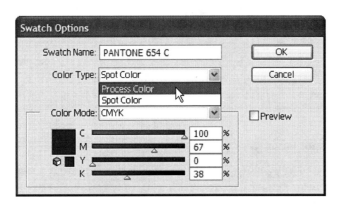

Exhibit 7-2: The Swatch Options dialog box

Tints

A tint is a lighter version of a base ink color. You can create a lighter version of a color by creating a tint, or a lower percentage of ink. When a color is printed at 100%, a solid layer of ink is applied. Any lower percentage uses a pattern of dots, or halftone screen, to simulate the percentage, rather than using an entirely different ink or inks. When you use a spot color, you can specify a tint in the Color panel by dragging the tint slider, as shown in Exhibit 7-3.

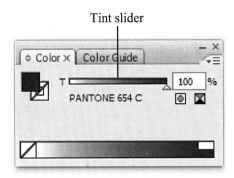

Exhibit 7-3: The Color panel with a spot color selected

Do it!

A-2: Adding swatches from a spot color library

Here's how	Here's why
1 Open **Outlander logo**	Located in the current unit folder.
Save the document as **My Outlander logo**	You'll include two spot colors to use in the logo. You want to add PANTONE 336 C and PANTONE 654 C.
ACE objective 3.1 2 In the Swatches panel, click the Swatch Libraries menu button	To expand the library list.
Choose **Color Books, PANTONE solid coated**	The PANTONE solid coated swatch library appears.
3 Display the panel menu	

	Point to the menu icon in the upper-right corner of the panel and click once.
From the menu, choose **Small List View**	The panel changes to show the names of the colors in addition to the color swatches.
4 From the panel menu, choose **Show Find Field**	A Find box appears in the panel.
Make sure students enter the number fluidly. If they pause between numbers, the wrong swatch will show up. 5 In the Find box, enter **336**	

	As you enter the number, the panel shows the color in the list.
6 Click **PANTONE 336 C** in the list of colors	A new swatch is added to the Swatches panel.
7 In the PANTONE solid coated swatch panel, find PANTONE 654 C	In the Find box, enter 654.

8	Add the spot color to the Swatches panel	Click PANTONE 654 C in the list of colors.
9	Close the PANTONE solid coated library panel	
10	On the artboard, select the text **Outlander**	Use the Selection tool to select the outlined text.
11	In the Tools panel, click the Stroke icon	
12	In the Swatches panel, click the PANTONE 336 C color swatch	To apply the spot color to the outlines of the text.
13	Apply the PANTONE 654 C color as a fill color for the **Spices** text	Select the "Spices" text, then click the Fill icon in the Tools panel and click the PANTONE 654 C color swatch.
14	Update the document	

Saving a swatch library

Explanation

You might want to save the colors in the Swatches panel as an external library. This is especially helpful if you know you'll be using the same colors a lot. Instead of having to import the colors from one document to another, you can open the library directly from the Swatches panel library list.

To save a swatch library:

1   In the Swatches panel, from the Swatch Libraries menu list, select Save Swatches to open the Save Swatches as Library dialog box.

2   Navigate to the location in which you want to save the library file. By default, the Swatches subfolder within the Documents and Settings folder is selected. If you save the new library in the Swatches folder, it will be available in the list of swatch libraries in Illustrator the next time you launch the application. If you save the library to a different location, you will need to navigate to that location each time you want to open the library.

3   In the File name box, enter a descriptive name for the library and click Save.

Do it!

A-3:   Saving a swatch library

Here's how	Here's why
1 From the Swatch Libraries menu list, select **Save Swatches...**	You'll save the colors you have in the Swatches panel so that you can access them easily when working in other documents.
2 Verify that the Swatches folder is visible	In the Documents and Settings folder.
3 In the File name box, enter **Outlander colors**	
Click **Save**	When you relaunch Illustrator, the color library will be available in the Swatch libraries menu list.
4 Update and close the document	
5 Close Illustrator; restart Illustrator	
6 Choose **File, Open Recent Files, My Outlander logo**	To open the logo document again.
7 From the Swatch Libraries menu list, select **User Defined, Outlander colors**	To open the saved Outlander colors swatch library. The Outlander colors swatch panel appears.
8 Close the Outlander colors swatch panel	

Topic B: Gradients

Explanation

One common way to make color more interesting is by applying gradients, which cause smooth transitions between multiple colors.

Create a basic gradient

To create and apply a gradient, use the Gradient panel, which is in the same panel group as the Stroke and Transparency panels.

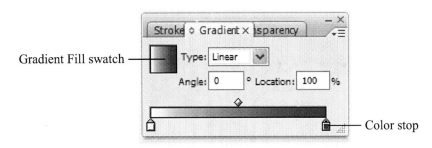

Exhibit 7-4: The Gradient panel

To create a gradient:

1   In the Gradient panel, select the Gradient Fill swatch. By default, a black and white gradient is visible.

2   To specify different colors to use in the gradient, click one of the color stops under the gradient bar, press Alt, and click a color in the Swatches panel. You can also drag a color from the Color panel or the Swatches panel to the color stop.

3   Follow the same procedure to define a second color for the gradient.

4   Select a gradient type, either Linear or Radial, from the Type list box. If you select Linear, you can specify the angle of the gradient in the Angle box. If you select Radial, the beginning color defines the center of the gradient fill, and the ending color defines the outer ring.

Do it!

B-1: Creating a new gradient

Here's how	Here's why
1 Select the four grouped leaves	You'll apply a gradient effect to the leaves.
2 In the panel dock, click ▣	To expand the Gradient panel.
3 Click the panel icon twice	(If necessary.) To expand the panel.
4 Click ▣	(The Gradient Fill swatch.) To apply the default gradient to the leaves. The white and black gradient runs left to right within each individual leaf. You'll create a green and white gradient.
5 Drag the PANTONE 336 C spot color swatch from the Swatches panel to the right color stop in the Gradient panel, as shown	The black color in the gradient changes to green. You'll add the gradient as a swatch in the Swatches panel.
6 In the Swatches panel, click the New Swatch button	To add the swatch and open the New Swatch dialog box.
7 In the Swatch Name box, enter **Green & White**	
Click **OK**	When you click OK, the panel changes to show only Gradient swatches.
8 Remove the black stroke from the leaves	In the Control panel, expand the Stroke list, then click the [None] color swatch.
9 Deselect the leaves	To view the results.
10 Update the document	

Adjusting gradients

After you've created a gradient, you might want to customize the colors, or alter the way it is applied to an item (or items). The following list describes some ways you can adjust gradients:

- To adjust the relative amount of a color in the gradient fill, drag the gradient slider along the gradient bar. As you drag the slider, the Location box automatically shows its location between the color stops. The default is 50, which indicates the slider is halfway between the two color stops. Dragging the slider either left or right alters the prominence of each color. (See Exhibit 7-5.)

- If you are working with a Linear gradient, enter a value in the Angle box to control the angle of the gradient.

- To create a gradient consisting of more than two colors, drag the additional colors anywhere below the gradient bar to create additional color stops. To delete a color stop, drag it outside the Gradient panel.

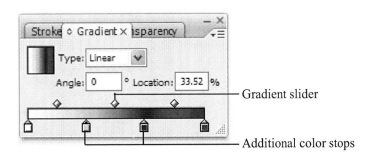

Exhibit 7-5: Adjusting a gradient by using the gradient slider

Adjusting gradients by using the Gradient tool

Although you can make many adjustments for gradients by using the Gradients panel, you can also use the Gradient tool to control how the gradient is applied to the item(s) in an illustration. You can use the Gradient tool to control the angle of the gradient, as well as the distance over which the gradient displays. For example, if you use the Gradient tool to drag over only a portion of an object, then the gradient blends across the distance you dragged, with the beginning color and ending color displaying as solid colors on either end of the area you dragged. In addition, if you begin dragging from outside the object and drag across and beyond the object, then only part of the gradient blend appears within the object.

In addition, you can use the Gradient tool to apply a gradient across multiple objects, as shown in Exhibit 7-6. For example, if you have a series of rectangles that you apply a gradient to, by default the gradient fills each rectangle. With the Gradient tool, you can spread the gradient across all of the objects.

Default application of a
gradient to multiple items

A gradient spread across multiple
items using the Gradient tool

Exhibit 7-6: An example of a gradient spread evenly across multiple items

Do it!

B-2: Adjusting a gradient

Here's how	Here's why
1 Select the four leaves	
2 In the Gradient panel, from the Type list, select **Radial**	The gradient in the leaves changes so that the colors expand outward from the center. Instead of the gradient being applied to each individual leaf, you want the colors to flow across all four leaves.
3 In the Tools panel, click	The Gradient tool.
4 Point to the center of the leaves, then drag out to the tip of one of the leaves	(The center is where the stems meet in the middle.) The gradient changes to flow across all four leaves. You'll also make the white color a little more prominent.
5 In the Gradient panel, drag the Gradient Slider to the right	
	Until the Location box reads about 75%.
6 Deselect the leaves	(In the Tools panel, select the Selection tool and click a blank area of the page.) To view the results.
7 Update the document	

Topic C: Transparency

This topic covers the following ACE exam objective for Illustrator CS3.

#	Objective
2.12	Modify overlapping objects by using the Transparency panel.

Applying transparency

Explanation

Another way to make illustrations more creative is to make items semi-transparent so that items that are behind can be partially seen. To do this, you need to work with the Transparency panel.

ACE objective 2.12

The Transparency panel

The Transparency panel contains an Opacity box as well as a list of blending modes you can use to adjust the transparency of selected items. The Transparency panel allows you to set the opacity of an object along a continuum from complete transparency on one end to full opacity on the other.

To change the opacity of items and make them transparent:

1 Select an item(s) with a fill applied.

2 In the Transparency panel, click the arrow to the right of the Opacity box to display the Opacity slider.

3 Drag the Opacity slider or enter a value in the Opacity box to specify the level of opacity as shown in Exhibit 7-7. The default opacity of objects is 100%, which means that they have 0% transparency. You can see a thumbnail image of the selected items on the panel. If it is not visible, you can click the Transparency panel tab two times, or choose Show Options from the panel menu to display the complete panel.

4 If desired, select a blending mode from the Blending Mode list.

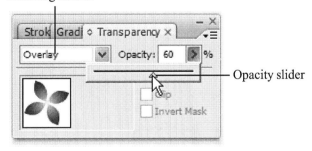

Exhibit 7-7: The Transparency panel

Blending modes

ACE objective 2.12

You can use blending modes to vary the ways that the colors of items blend with the colors of underlying items. When you apply a blending mode to an item, the effect of the blending mode is seen on any items that lie beneath the item's layer or group. The following table describes the blending mode options in the Transparency panel.

Option	Description
Normal	Fills the selection with the blend color, without interaction with the base color. This is the default mode.
Darken	Selects the base or blend color (whichever is darker) as the resulting color. Areas lighter than the blend color are replaced. Areas darker than the blend color do not change.
Multiply	Multiplies the base color by the blend color. The resulting color is always a darker color.
Color Burn	Darkens the base color to reflect the blend color.
Lighten	Selects the base or blend color (whichever is lighter) as the resulting color. Areas darker than the blend color are replaced. Areas lighter than the blend color do not change.
Screen	Multiplies the inverse of the blend and base colors. The resulting color is always a lighter color.
Color Dodge	Brightens the base color to reflect the blend color.
Overlay	Multiplies or screens the colors, depending on the base color. Patterns or colors overlay the existing artwork.
Soft Light	Darkens or lightens the colors, depending on the blend color. The effect is similar to shining a diffused spotlight on the artwork.
Hard Light	Multiplies or screens the colors, depending on the blend color. The effect is similar to shining a harsh spotlight on the artwork.
Difference	Subtracts either the blend color from the base color or the base color from the blend color, depending on which has the greater brightness value.
Exclusion	Creates an effect similar to, but lower in contrast than, the Difference mode.
Hue	Creates a resulting color with the luminance and saturation of the base color and the hue of the blend color.
Saturation	Creates a resulting color with the luminance and hue of the base color and the saturation of the blend color.
Color	Creates a resulting color with the luminance of the base color and the hue and saturation of the blend color.
Luminosity	Creates a resulting color with the hue and saturation of the base color and the luminance of the blend color. This mode creates an inverse effect from that of the Color mode.

Do it!

C-1: Setting transparency

ACE objective 2.12

Here's how	Here's why
1 In the panel dock, click ⊘	To view the Transparency panel. You'll adjust the transparency of the leaves so that the text "Outlander" shows through from behind.
2 Select the four leaves	
3 In the Transparency panel, on the right side of the Opacity box, click to view the opacity slider	
Drag the slider to the left to approximately 75%	You'll also adjust the blending mode so that the text shows through a little clearer.
4 From the blending modes list, select **Overlay**	
5 Deselect the leaves	To view the results.
6 Update and close the document	

Unit summary: Working with fills and colors

Topic A   In this topic, you learned to **import swatch libraries** from other documents, **open preset swatch libraries**, and **export colors in the Swatches panel as a new custom library**.

Topic B   In this topic, you learned to **create and apply gradients** to items in an illustration. You also **adjusted a gradient** by changing its angle and applying it evenly to multiple items.

Topic C   In this topic, you learned to **adjust the opacity** for an item by using the **Transparency panel**. This included **applying a blending mode** so that the color of underlying items mixed with the overlapping items.

Independent practice activity

In this activity, you'll open a spot color swatch library, and add a spot color to an illustration. You'll apply the spot color to certain objects, then you'll use it to create a color gradient.

1 Open the Chicken recipe_fills practice document (located in the current unit folder). Save the document as My chicken recipe_fills practice.

2 Open the PANTONE solid coated spot color library. (*Hint*: Choose Window, Swatch Libraries to view the list of swatch libraries. PANTONE colors are under Color Books)

3 Locate the PANTONE 5535 C spot color swatch and add the swatch to the Swatches panel. (*Hint*: From the PANTONE solid coated panel menu, choose Show Find Field, and enter 5535 in the Find box. Click the swatch to add it to the Swatches panel.)

4 Close the PANTONE solid coated swatch panel, apply the PANTONE 5535 C color to the stroke of the large rectangle surrounding the recipe. (*Hint*: Select the rectangle and click the PANTONE 5535 C swatch in the Swatches panel.)

5 Select the green star near the right side of the recipe and apply a gradient to the star using PANTONE 5535 C and white. (*Hint*: In the Gradient panel, click the Gradient Fill swatch. Drag the PANTONE 5535 C swatch from the Swatches panel to the right color stop, and the white swatch to the left color stop. If necessary, remove excess color stops by dragging them down off the panel.)

6 Adjust the gradient so that it is a radial gradient and drag the gradient slider so that white is the prominent color. (*Hint*: From the Type list, select Radial. Drag the gradient slider to the right to make the white color more prominent.)

7 Update and close the document.

Review questions

1 A color printed with a single pre-mixed ink is called a _____ color.

   spot

2 To create a lighter version of a base color, drag the _____ slider for that color in the Color panel.

   Tint

3 How can you convert a process color swatch to a spot color?

   A Double-click the process color swatch to open the Swatch Options dialog box, and then choose Spot Color from the Color Type list.

   B Right-click the process color swatch, and then choose Convert To Spot Color from the pop-up menu.

   C Select the process color swatch you want to convert, and then choose Convert To Spot Color from the panel menu.

   D Select the process color swatch you want to convert, and then choose Edit, Convert To Spot Color.

4 You have the PANTONE Solid Coated swatch library open, and you want to locate the PANTONE 654 C spot color. What is the most effective way to search for the color?

   A Select one of the spot color swatches and type 654 to jump to the color you want.

   B Point to one of the spot color swatches to view its name; then continue the process until you find the color you want.

   C From the panel menu, choose Show Find Field, and in the Find box enter 654.

   D From the panel menu, choose List View to view the names of all the spot color swatches, and scroll through the list to find the color you want.

5 You have an object with a white and black gradient fill applied to it. You want the gradient to be white and green. How can you change the black color in the gradient to green?

   A In the Gradient panel, click the black color stop, and then select a green color in the Swatches panel.

   B Drag a green color from the Swatches panel to the black color stop in the Gradient panel.

   C In the Gradient panel, right-click the black color stop, and then choose a green color from the drop-down list of swatches.

   D Drag a green color swatch from the Swatches panel to the black area of the shape containing the gradient.

6 True or false? A gradient can contain more than two colors.

   True

7 To adjust the starting and ending point of a gradient (for example, to make one gradient flow across multiple selected shapes), you should use the _____.

Gradient tool

8 You want to adjust the opacity for a selected object so that an underlying object becomes partially visible. You should:

A In the Color panel, adjust the color percentage sliders until you achieve the effect you want.

B In the Transparency panel, adjust the Opacity slider until you achieve the effect you want.

C In the Color panel, double-click the fill color icon; then in the dialog box adjust the Opacity slider until you achieve the effect you want.

D Choose Object, Flatten Transparency; then adjust the Opacity slider until you achieve the effect you want.

9 To change how an item's colors interact with the colors of underlying items, choose a _____.

blending mode

10 You have made an overlapping object opaque by adjusting the Opacity slider in the Transparency panel, but you also want to adjust the way colors are blended. Which are valid blending modes you can choose from? (Choose all the apply.)

A Multiply

B Darken

C Color Burn

D Intensity

Unit 8

Adjusting typography

Unit time: 50 minutes

Complete this unit, and you'll know how to:

A Convert shapes to type containers, link two or more containers so that text flows through them, and wrap text around the edges of a graphic.

B Set and format tab markers in text, insert typographic characters, and use character and paragraph styles to quickly apply specific formatting to text.

C Check spelling in text, find and replace text throughout an entire illustration, and use the Find Font dialog box to quickly view and adjust which fonts are used in an illustration.

Topic A: Flow type

This topic covers the following ACE exam objective for Illustrator CS3.

#	Objective
4.8	Given a scenario, choose the appropriate option for dealing with legacy text. (Scenarios include: open file and update all legacy text, update all, update one, exporting to legacy Illustrator versions.)

Import text

Explanation

When you import a large amount of text, you might want to split the text up so that it flows through different parts of an illustration. This could be either because the type is too long for the area in which you originally imported it, or you want to split the text up for design purposes. You also might want to force text to flow around certain objects in the illustration.

Link type containers

Although you can cut and paste text to move it to other parts of an illustration, a more efficient way to manage the body text is by linking multiple type containers so that the text automatically flows through them. With linked type containers, you can resize the containers so that the text flows the way you want.

Each type container contains two ports; one near the upper-left corner of the container, and one near the lower-right corner. The icons in the ports indicate whether there is hidden text or whether the container is linked to other containers. A blank port at the beginning of a type container indicates the beginning of the text. A port with a red plus sign at the end of a type container indicates there is additional hidden text, as shown in Exhibit 8-1. A port with a small arrow indicates the type container is linked to another type container (see Exhibit 8-2), and a blank port at the end of a container indicates all the text is visible.

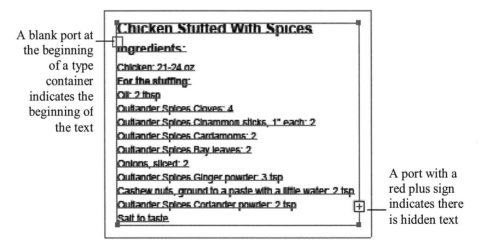

Exhibit 8-1: A type container with hidden text

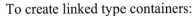

To create linked type containers:

1 Use the Selection tool to select the type container that contains the overflow text. Type containers that contain hidden text show a small red plus sign in the lower-right port.

2 Click the red plus sign in the lower-right port of the container. The pointer changes to a small page icon, indicating it is "loaded" with the text you want to link.

3 Click another type container, or click the border of a closed shape (to convert the shape to a type container). As you release the mouse button, the link is set between the two containers, and the text, which was hidden, appears in the linked type container. Also, if text threads are visible, a blue line shows the link between the two containers. (You might have to choose View, Show Text Threads to see the blue line.)

4 Continue linking type containers until all the text is visible. When a type container no longer contains hidden text, an empty port shows in the lower-right corner, as shown in Exhibit 8-2.

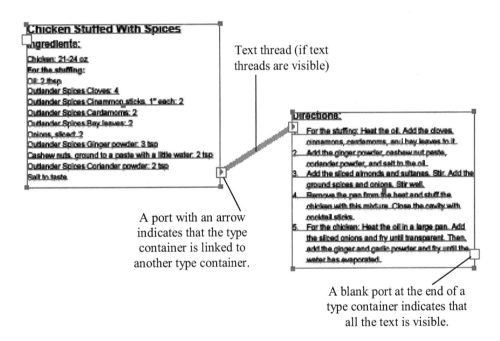

Exhibit 8-2: An example of linked type containers

Linking multiple type containers simultaneously

If you already have placeholders for the text in an illustration, you can simultaneously link multiple type containers by selecting all the containers (or shapes to be converted to type containers) and choosing Type, Threaded Text, Create. The items are then linked in the order they were created.

Manipulating text threads

You can unlink type containers, re-direct the order in which the containers are linked, or remove all threads and have the text stay in place. Start by selecting a linked type container, and then do one of the following:

- To re-direct the thread between linked type containers, click the lower-right port on the type container from where you want to redirect the link. This loads the pointer, and it changes to a small page icon. Click the new type container where you want the link to go.

- To break the thread between two containers, double-click the port at the beginning of the second container. The first container shows a red plus sign indicating it has hidden text again.

- To release a type container from a thread, choose Type, Threaded Text, Release Selection. The text flows into the next linked container.

- To remove all threads, choose Type, Threaded Text, Remove Threading. The text stays in place, but the containers are no longer linked.

Do it!   **A-1:   Linking type containers**

Here's how	Here's why
1 Open **Recipes_typography**	Located in the current unit folder.
Save the document as **My recipes_typography**	You'll import the recipes text so that it flows through the four rectangles on the artboard.
2 In the Tools panel, select the Type tool	
3 Click one of the edges of the top-left rectangle	*ipes of t* To convert the rectangle to a type container.
4 Import the **Recipes text** Word document	Choose File, Place and navigate to the current unit folder. Select Recipes text and click Place. In the Microsoft Word Options dialog box, verify that Remove Text Formatting is clear, and click OK.
5 Press and hold CTRL	To temporarily select the Selection tool.
Click the text	To select the type container.
6 Observe the type container	A small red plus sign (+) is visible in the lower-right corner, indicating there is additional hidden text.
7 While pressing CTRL, point to the small red +	Pressing Ctrl temporarily selects the Selection tool, which is necessary in order to click the red plus sign.
Click once, move the pointer away from the red +, and release CTRL	The pointer now includes a small page icon with text.

8 Point to one of the edges of the bottom-left rectangle

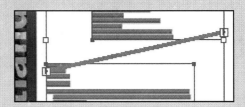

When the pointer is over the edge of the rectangle, the page icon changes slightly.

Click one of the edges of the bottom-left rectangle

The rectangle converts to a type container, and more of the text is visible.

9 Choose **View, Show Text Threads**

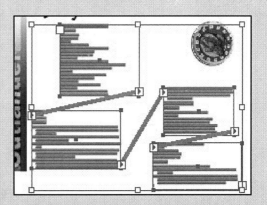

A thick line appears from the end of the previous type container to the current type container as a visual indicator that they are linked.

10 Flow the text through the remaining two rectangles

Flow the text through the top-right rectangle, then the bottom-right rectangle. (Click the red +, and click one of the edges of the top-right rectangle. Repeat for the bottom-right rectangle.)

11 Click a blank area of the artboard

To deselect the type containers.

12 Click the top-left type container	To select it. You'll resize the type container to include the entire list of ingredients for the chicken recipe.
Drag the bottom-center handle of the type container down	

	Until the items in the list of ingredients are together. The next linked type container should begin with the text "Directions:"
13 Choose **View, Hide Text Threads**	To hide the text threads.
14 Deselect the type container	To view the results.
15 Update the document	

Legacy text

Explanation

ACE objective 4.8

Any documents created with Illustrator version 10 or prior are referred to as *legacy* documents. You can open legacy documents in CS3, but in order to edit any text within them, you need to update them. There are several ways you can deal with legacy text updates. You can:

- Open the document without updating the text. This is the easiest option if you know you don't need to edit the text. When you open the document, the text blocks will still look correct, but they will have an "x" through them when you select them, indicating that they can't be edited. However, you can still reposition the text blocks, and the text will still print correctly.

- Update all the text when you open the document. If you choose this option, Illustrator will likely reflow the text, but the changes should be minor. Once the text is updated, you can manipulate it any way you want.

- Open the document without updating the text, and then update only the text blocks you need to edit. To update specific text blocks, select the blocks you want to update, then choose Type, Legacy Text, Update Selected Text. You can also choose whether to create a copy of the legacy text below the updated text for comparison. Once you've finished your edits, you can delete the copy of the legacy text.

To update legacy documents:

1 Open the legacy document you want to convert. When you do, a dialog box appears alerting you that the document contains legacy text, as shown in Exhibit 8-3.

2 To update all of the legacy text, click Update.

3 To update the legacy text later on, click OK.

4 To cancel opening the file, click Cancel.

When Illustrator opens the legacy document, it adds the name "Converted" to the file name. Documents created with Illustrator CS or CS2 open in CS3 without requiring any updates.

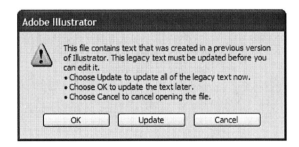

Exhibit 8-3: Legacy text alert dialog box

Do it!

A-2:   Updating legacy text

ACE objective 4.8

Here's how	Here's why
1 Open **Web page_typography**	Located in the current unit folder. This document was created in Illustrator 10, so a dialog box appears alerting you that the legacy text needs to be updated in order for you to edit it.
2 Click **OK**	**Featured Product** Since 600 B.C., the brilliantly yelloww-colored turmeric has been widely used for dyeing, medicines, and flavoring. It comes To open the document without updating the text. The document opens, and the text appears fine. However, you realize there is a typo in the first sentence under the Featured Product heading. The word "yelloww" has an extra "w".
3 Using the Selection tool, click the paragraph below the Featured Product heading	To select it. Each line of text has an "x" through it, indicating that the legacy text still needs to be updated before you can edit it.
4 Choose **Type**, **Legacy Text**, **Update Selected Legacy Text**	
5 Select the text again	The x's are gone and the text is editable, so you can now fix the typo.
6 Using the Text tool, fix the typo in the word "yelloww" in the first sentence	
7 Save and close the document	When Illustrator prompts you for a file name, use the default and click Save.

Wrap text around items

Explanation

Often you'll combine text and images in an illustration so that they complement each other. For example, you might want text to flow around the shape of an image, similar to the example in Exhibit 8-4. By default, when you overlap text and images or text and vector shapes, the text will either be on top of the items or behind the items. To fix this, you can force text to wrap around items by using the Make Text Wrap command.

Exhibit 8-4: An example of an item that has text wrap applied (with text wrap boundaries visible)

To wrap text around an item:

1 Use the Selection tool to select the item you want the text to wrap around.

2 If necessary, bring the selected item in front of the text in the stacking order. Text will not wrap to an item if it is behind the text.

3 Choose Object, Text Wrap, Make Text Wrap.

If you want to release the text wrap, select the item, and choose Object, Text Wrap, Release Text Wrap.

Edit a text wrap

After you have wrapped text around an item, you might want to adjust the amount of space between the edges of the item and the text. By default, Illustrator generates six points of space for the text wrap, similar to the amount of space shown in Exhibit 8-4. To adjust the amount the text is offset, verify the item used in the text wrap is selected, and choose Object, Text Wrap, Text Wrap Options. In the corresponding dialog box, shown in Exhibit 8-5, you can increase or decrease the amount of space, or invert the text wrap, which wraps the text around the opposite side of the item.

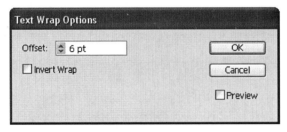

Exhibit 8-5: The Text Wrap Options dialog box

Do it!

A-3:   **Wrapping text**

Here's how	Here's why
1 Use the Selection tool to position the chicken image on the left side of the chicken recipe ingredients text, as shown	
	You'll wrap the ingredients for the chicken recipe so that the text flows around the right side of the plate.
2 Choose **Object, Text Wrap, Make**	
	The text wraps around the curve of the plate and automatically uses the clipping mask circle you created earlier, not the edges of the image.
3 Zoom in on the chicken image	So that you can see the list of ingredients clearly. You'll add more space between the curve of the plate and the text.
4 Choose **Object, Text Wrap, Text Wrap Options...**	To open the Text Wrap Options dialog box.
5 Move the dialog box	(If necessary.) To clearly see the circle.
6 In the Offset box, click the up arrow four times	To increase the amount of space between the text and the hidden circle. (The Offset box should show 10 pts.)
7 Check **Preview**	To view the increase in the illustration.
Click **OK**	

Tell students to leave this file open because it will be used later.

8 View the entire artboard

9 Deselect any items, and update the document

Topic B: Format text

This topic covers the following ACE exam objectives for Illustrator CS3.

#	Objective
4.1	List and describe the advantages and disadvantages when using OpenType, True-Type, or Type 1 fonts.
4.3	Manage the composition of text by using panels, menus, and preferences settings.
4.4	Create and modify type by using Character and Paragraph styles.
4.7	Insert special characters by using the Type menu and the Glyphs panel.

Tabs and styles

Explanation

After you have body text added to an illustration, there are certain aspects of the text that you will likely want to change. You might need to reset any tabs in the text, or you might want to consistently format the text with new formatting options.

Tabs

You'll begin by learning how to set and adjust tabs to align text horizontally within single lines or paragraphs. It is often easiest to type tab characters into the text prior to setting tab stops so that you can see the results as you set them. After you have entered the tabs you want in the text, you can format them by using the Tabs panel.

In Illustrator, you can specify four types of tabs. The following table describes the four tab styles.

Button	Name	Description
⬇	Left-Justified Tab	Aligns horizontal text to the right of the tab mark.
⬇	Center-Justified Tab	Centers text on the tab mark.
⬇	Right-Justified Tab	Aligns horizontal text to the left of the tab mark.
⬇	Decimal-Justified Tab	Aligns numbers at the decimal point.

ACE objective 4.3

To add tab stops and adjust tabs for existing tab characters:

1   Choose Window, Type, Tabs to open the Tab panel ruler, as shown in Exhibit 8-6.

2   If necessary, using one of the type tools, select a range of text or place the insertion point in the desired location. If you want to adjust tabs for an entire type container, select the type container with the Selection tool before you open the Tab panel.

3   Select the desired Tab Style button (described in the above table).

4   On the Tab Ruler, click where you want the tab marker to appear.

5   To adjust the tab marker, drag it to the left or right on the tab ruler. If you want to precisely position a tab marker, verify that the tab marker is selected on the tab ruler; then enter a value in the Tab position box.

6   If you want to apply a leader for a tab, verify the tab marker is selected on the tab ruler; then enter the leader you want in the Leader box.

7   If you are working with a Decimal Justified tab, you can indicate a specific character for the tab to align with by entering the character in the Align On box. You can type or paste any character, but you need to make sure that the paragraphs you're aligning contain that character.

8   To close the Tab panel, click the close button in the upper-right corner.

You can also delete a tab, repeat a tab, and clear all the tabs by choosing the appropriate commands from the Tabs panel menu.

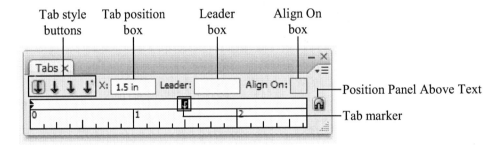

Exhibit 8-6: The Tabs panel

Sometimes you might accidentally move the Tabs panel, or you might change the magnification so that the text and the Tabs panel no longer line up. You can quickly reposition the Tabs panel with the text by clicking the Position Panel Above Text icon near the right side of the panel.

Do it!

B-1:   Setting tabs

Here's how	Here's why
1 Open **Starter set_typography** Save the file as **My starter set_typography**	Located in the current unit folder.
2 Import the Starter spices Word document, using the large rectangle as a type container	(Select the Type tool and click the border of the large rectangle to convert it to a type container. Choose File, Place, navigate to the current unit folder, and choose Starter spices. Keep the same formatting applied in the Word document.)
3 Zoom in on the text	So that it is clearly visible. You'll format the text, starting with setting tabs so that the prices for each spice are right-aligned.
4 Using the Selection tool, click the text	(If necessary.) To select the type container.
5 Choose **Window**, **Type**, **Tabs**	To open the Tabs panel, which appears at the top of the type container.
6 Click just above the 4-inch mark	 To create a new tab marker. The prices shift to the 4-inch mark. You'll adjust the tab so that the prices are more to the right.
7 Drag the tab marker to the 5-inch mark	You might need to expand the Tab panel first. The spice prices shift to the 5-inch mark. You want the prices to be right-aligned.
8 Click	(The Right-Justified Tab button.) The prices are right-aligned, but still need to be more to the right. You'll align them precisely to the 5¼-inch mark.
9 Edit the value in the X box to **5.25** Press ↵ ENTER	You'll also apply a leader.
10 In the Leader box, enter **.** Press ↵ ENTER	A period.

ACE objective 4.3

Students can also press Shift+Ctrl+T to open Tabs.

Let students know the text already has the tabs added. That is why the prices shift automatically.

TIPS *Let students know they can also choose Snap to Unit from the Tabs panel menu to automatically snap tab markers to the nearest ruler units.*

11	Deselect the text	(Click a blank area of the artboard.) A dotted line now shows from the spice headings to the corresponding prices.
	Close the Tabs panel	
12	Update the document	

Typographic characters

Explanation

You can insert typographic characters such as fractions or other special characters. Often you can insert special symbols by holding down the Alt key and typing a code from the numeric keypad, although to do this you need to know the code for the character you want. Instead of remembering or looking up character codes, you can use the Glyphs panel to easily insert special characters.

Glyphs

ACE objective 4.7

A *glyph* is the shape representing a character. A glyph character can be an ordinary number or letter, for example the letter "A," or a variation of the letter or number. For example the capital letter "A" might be available in a small cap or swash form. Glyphs can be a special character such as the cent symbol. A typeface might contain just standard representations of letters and numbers, or might provide a large selection of alternative forms and special characters.

To insert typographic characters:

1   Choose Window, Type, Glyphs to open the Glyphs panel, which is shown in Exhibit 8-7. (You can also choose Type, Glyphs to open the panel.)

2   Using the Type tool, click where you want to insert the character.

3   If you want to use a character from another font, select the font from the Font and Font Style lists at the bottom of the panel.

4   Double-click the glyph to add it at the location of the insertion point.

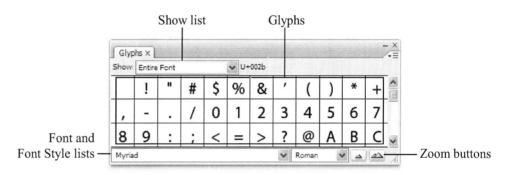

Exhibit 8-7: The Glyphs panel

OpenType fonts

ACE objective 4.1

Typically, most fonts included with a computer's operating system are either TrueType or Type 1 PostScript fonts. However, if you have OpenType fonts available, you can make use of their expanded capabilities. *OpenType* is a font format that uses a single font file for both Macintosh and Windows computers. OpenType fonts contain many characters not available in other font types, including fractions, small caps, superscript and subscript characters, swashes, and more.

When working with OpenType fonts, you can automatically substitute alternate glyphs, such as ligatures, small capitals, fractions, and old style proportional figures, in your text. In Illustrator, these options are available in the OpenType panel, shown in Exhibit 8-8.

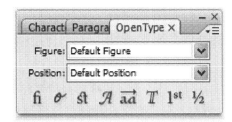

Exhibit 8-8: The OpenType panel

In addition to the options in the OpenType panel, the Glyphs panel will also show expanded characters. If you have an OpenType font selected, small black triangles might be visible in the lower-right corner of some glyphs, which indicates that a list of alternate glyphs is available.

OpenType fonts with support for central European (CE) languages can be distinguished by the word "Pro," at the end of the font name in the Fonts list. OpenType fonts that don't contain central European language support are labeled "Std" (Standard) in the Font list. All OpenType fonts can be installed and used alongside Type 1 PostScript and TrueType fonts.

To format type by using the OpenType panel:

1   Choose Window, Type, OpenType to open the OpenType panel.

2   With the Type tool, select the type to which you want to apply alternate characters.

3   In the OpenType panel, click a button to apply ligatures, swashes, ordinals, fractions, or other alternate characters. (If the font applied to the type is not an OpenType font, the options are not available.)

Do it!

B-2:   Inserting typographic characters

Here's how	Here's why
1 Choose **Window, My recipes_typography.ai**	To return to the recipes document.
2 Zoom in on the cooking directions for the chicken recipe	(The lower-left type container.) In the second step, the word "Saute" should have an accent over the letter "e."

ACE objective 4.7

3 Select the letter **e** in the word **Saute**	2. Add the gir Saut**e** until 3. Add the sli

TIPS *You can also choose Type, Glyphs to open the Glyphs panel.*

4 Choose **Window, Type, Glyphs**	To open the Glyphs panel.
5 Scroll down in the list of glyphs to view the **e** characters with varying accents over them	*(Glyphs panel showing: ~ Ä Å Ç É Ñ Ö Ü á à â ä / ã å ç é è ê ë í ì î ï ñ / ó ò ô ö õ ú ù û ü † ° ¢ — Arial Regular)*
6 Double-click the first accented letter **e** as shown	*(Glyphs panel showing: Å Ç É Ñ Ö / ç é è ê ë / ô ö õ ú ù)* To add the accented "é" to the word "Sauté."
7 Using the Selection tool, press and hold (SPACEBAR) and then drag to the left	To scroll to the right side of the artboard to view the list of ingredients for the potatoes recipe. The fraction ½ in the first line is not formatted correctly. You'll insert a glyph so that the fraction looks correct.
8 Using the Type tool, select the unformatted fraction **½** in the first line of the ingredients text	and quartered: 2 **1/2** cups to a paste with a little wat
9 Scroll down in the list of glyphs to view the available fractions	In the Glyphs panel.
10 Double-click **½**	*(Glyphs panel showing: ž ¦ Đ ð Ý / ³ ½ ¼ ¾ Ⅎ / Č č đ — ·)* Lastly, you'll add a copyright symbol to the disclaimer at the bottom of the illustration.

11 Using the Selection tool, press (SPACEBAR) and drag up	To view the disclaimer at the bottom of the artboard.
12 Using the Type tool, place the insertion point to the left of **Outlander**	"Outlander" is the first word in the line of text located at the bottom of the artboard.
13 Scroll down in the list of glyphs to view the copyright symbol	
14 Double-click the copyright symbol	
Press (SPACEBAR)	(If necessary.) To add a space after the symbol.
15 View the entire artboard and close the Glyphs panel	
Update the document	

Styles

Explanation

You can ensure consistent formatting for the text by using character and paragraph styles. A *style* is a collection of character and paragraph formatting attributes that are saved together as a group, and can be applied to other portions of text in a document. Styles allow you to format a document efficiently and consistently, because you can select a specific portion of text, a paragraph, or a group of paragraphs, and select a style to apply all the formatting in a single step.

You can create paragraph styles or character styles. *Character styles* include only character formatting and are applied to specific portions of text. *Paragraph styles* can include character and paragraph formatting, and always apply to entire paragraphs, even if you have only a portion of the paragraph selected.

Create styles

ACE objective 4.4

To create styles, you need to work in either the Character Styles panel (shown in Exhibit 8-9) or the Paragraph Styles panel. Both panels are very similar and include a list of styles (if any exist) as well as buttons for creating and deleting styles. You can create a style based on formatting applied to existing type, or you can create a new style from scratch.

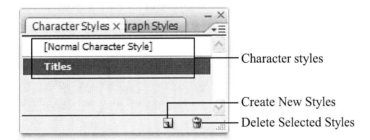

Exhibit 8-9: The Character Styles panel

To create a style based on the formatting of existing type:

1 Select the text. It contains the formatting that you'll base your style on.

2 If necessary, choose Window, Type, Character Styles or Paragraph Styles to open either the Character Styles panel or the Paragraph Styles panel.

3 Press and hold Alt, and then in the panel, click the Create New Style button. Pressing Alt as you click automatically opens the Character Style Options dialog box (shown in Exhibit 8-10) or the Paragraph Style Options dialog box. Each dialog box shows options for the type of style you are creating.

4 In the Style Name box, enter a name for the style. The General category on the left side of the dialog box shows information about the current formatting used in the style.

5 If you want to change the formatting used in the style, select a new category, and make the formatting changes in the style settings section.

6 Click OK to create the style.

Style categories

Style Name box

Style settings

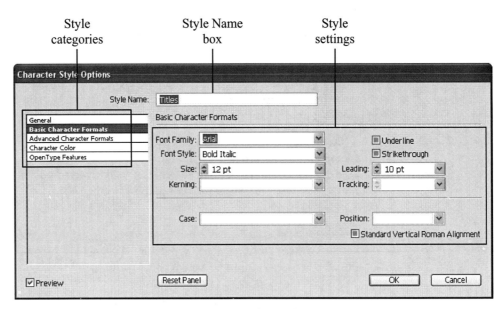

Exhibit 8-10: The Character Style Options dialog box

Apply styles

To apply a style to text, select the text you want to format with the style, and click the style in the panel. For character styles, you need to select all the text you want to format with the style. For paragraph styles, you need to select only a portion of a paragraph to apply the style to the entire paragraph. You can also select portions of multiple paragraphs.

A plus sign might appear next to the style name in the panel. This indicates that there are overrides to the style. An override is any formatting that does not match the attributes defined by the style. There are several ways to remove style overrides:

- To clear overrides and return text to the appearance defined by the style, reapply the same style or choose Clear Overrides from the panel menu.

- To clear overrides while applying a style, press and hold Alt as you click the style name.

You can also delete a style (with the exception of the default style). To do so, first select the style you want to delete; then click the Delete Selected Style button.

Modify styles

Sometimes you might want to modify a style after you've been using it for a while. To modify a style:

1   In the Character Styles or Paragraph Styles panel, double-click the style you want to modify. The Character Style Options or Paragraph Style Options dialog box appears.

2   Specify new settings or modify the existing settings.

3   Click OK to close the dialog box and apply the changes. When you modify a style, the text to which you have already applied the style updates to reflect the new settings.

Do it!   **B-3:   Using character styles**

Here's how	Here's why
1 Choose **Window, My starter set_typography.ai**	To return to the starter set artboard.
2 Using the Type tool, select the first spice heading as shown	Cinnamon Cinnamon is one of role in baked goods Nutmeg Nutmeg comes from
	(Double-click the word "Cinnamon" to select it.) You'll format all the spice headings so they are bolder. To do this, you'll create and apply a character style.
3 Format the text as 12 pt, Bold, Italic	(In the Control panel, choose Bold Italic from the Font Style list, and 12 pt from the Font Size list.)
	You'll create a character style based on the selected text for the remaining headings.
ACE objective 4.4 4 Choose **Window, Type, Character Styles**	To open the Character Styles panel.
5 Press ⟮ALT⟯ and click	(The Create New Style button.) To create a new style and automatically open the Character Style Options dialog box. (If you don't press Alt as you click the button, you will need to double-click the new style in the Character Styles panel to open the dialog box.)
6 In the Style Name box, edit the style name to read **Titles**	
7 Observe the Style Settings pane	Style Settings: [Normal Character Style] + ▽ Basic Character Formats Font Family:Arial Font Style:Bold Italic Size: 12 pt Leading: 12 pt ▽ Advanced Character Formats
	The pane shows a summary of the formatting applied to the text.
8 On the left side, click **Basic Character Formats**	The right pane changes to show options you can use to continue formatting the style. You'll leave the current settings as they are.
Click **OK**	To close the dialog box. The character style shows in the Character Styles panel.

9	Use the Type tool to select the second spice heading, as shown	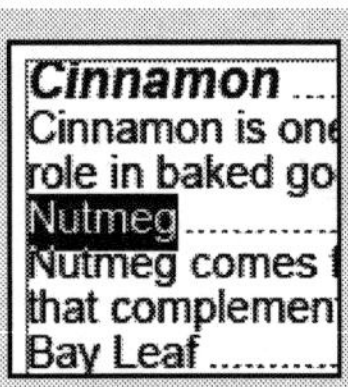 Cinnamon Cinnamon is one role in baked go Nutmeg Nutmeg comes that complemen Bay Leaf
		Double-click the word "Nutmeg."
10	In the Character Styles panel, click **Titles**	The text does not appear to change and a small plus sign appears next to the character style. This indicates that the local formatting is overriding the character style settings. You'll force the text to use the character style settings.
11	In the Character Styles panel, click **Titles** a second time	The small plus sign disappears, and the text shows the style formatting. You can also press Alt as you click a style to automatically override local formatting without having to click the style twice.
12	Use the Type tool to select the third spice heading	The Bay Leaf heading.
13	Press (ALT) and click **Titles**	In the Character Styles panel.
14	Format the remaining spice headings with the **Titles** character style	The headings are Cloves, Cumin, Star Anise, Pepper, and Coriander.
15	Deselect the text and update the document	

Paragraph styles

Explanation

ACE objective 4.4

Paragraph styles work exactly the same way as character styles, except the formatting you specify for paragraph styles applies to entire paragraphs instead of specific portions of text. Paragraph styles include leading values, paragraph alignment, and indentation settings as well as any character formatting.

Do it!

B-4:   Using paragraph styles

Here's how	Here's why
1 Use the Type tool to place the insertion point in the second paragraph, as shown	*Cinnamon* Cinnamon is one of th role in baked goods ar *Nutmeg* Nutmeg comes from th (The paragraph just below the Cinnamon heading.) You'll indent the text and add some space below it. To do this you'll create and apply a paragraph style.
2 In the Control panel, expand the Paragraph drop-down panel	Click the blue Paragraph link to view the drop-down panel.
3 In the Left Indent box, enter **10**	
4 In the Right Indent box, enter **50**	
5 In the Space after paragraph box, enter **10**	
Press (↵ ENTER)	To apply the changes and close the drop-down panel. You'll now create a paragraph style based on the formatting.
6 Activate the Paragraph Styles panel	In the Character Styles panel group, click the Paragraph Styles tab.
7 Press (ALT) and click [▣]	(The Create New Style button.) The Paragraph Style Options dialog box automatically appears.
8 In the Style Name box, enter **Descriptions**	
9 Observe the Style Settings pane	Similar to character styles, the pane shows a summary of the formatting applied to the text.
10 On the left side, click **Basic Character Formats**	The right pane changes to show options you can use to continue formatting the style.

Remind students that they do not need to select the entire paragraph to apply paragraph formatting.

ACE objective 4.4

11	From the Leading list, select **10 pt** Click **OK**	To reduce the default 12 pt leading.
12	Click to place the insertion point in the fourth paragraph, as shown	*Cinnamon* .... Cinnamon is one and prominent rol in stews and sauc *Nutmeg* .... Nutmeg comes from aromatic flavor that baked goods. The paragraph just below the Nutmeg heading.
13	Press (ALT) and click **Descriptions**	In the Paragraph Styles panel. (Pressing Alt forces the style to override local formatting applied to the text.)
14	Format the remaining description paragraphs	
15	Close the Paragraph Styles panel	
16	Deselect the text, and view the entire artboard	
17	Update the document	

Topic C: Edit text

This topic covers the following ACE exam objective for Illustrator CS3.

#	Objective
4.3	Manage the composition of text by using panels, menus, and preferences settings.

Explanation

When you work with text in an illustration, you will likely want to perform basic text editing procedures to ensure the text is spelled correctly and uses the fonts you intended, or you might need to replace a word or a portion of text that is used multiple times in the text. There are options in Illustrator you can use to ensure the text is accurate.

Checking spelling

You can correct any misspelled words in an illustration by using the Check Spelling command. The Check Spelling command will not flag any spelling errors for text that's been converted to outlines. If you have a lot of text you're going to convert to outlines, you should run the spelling checker before you convert the text.

ACE objective 4.3

To check spelling in an illustration:

1 Choose Edit, Check Spelling to open the Check Spelling dialog box, as shown in Exhibit 8-11.

2 If necessary, click the arrow icon at the lower-left corner of the dialog box to view and change parameters for the spelling check.

3 Click Start to start checking the text for incorrectly spelled words. Incorrect spellings appear in the Word Not Found box. Alternative spellings for each misspelled word appear in the Suggestions box.

4 Change any misspellings by using the available options:

   • Select the correctly spelled word in the Suggestions box and click Change. You can also click Change All to change all occurrences of the suspect word in the illustration.

   • Type the correct spelling for the word in the Word Not Found box and click Change.

   • Click Add to add a suspect word to the dictionary.

   • Click Ignore or Ignore All to continue checking spelling without changing a suspect word.

5 Click Done to close the Check Spelling dialog box.

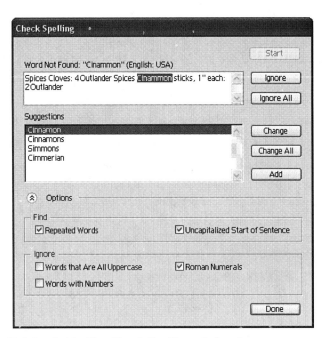

Exhibit 8-11: The Check Spelling dialog box

Do it!

C-1: Proofing text

ACE objective 4.3

Make sure students do not have any type containers selected before they open the Check Spelling dialog box.

If this is not the first time you've keyed the course on this computer, the word could already be "added" to the dictionary and thus not flagged.

Here's how	Here's why
1 Choose **Edit**, **Check Spelling...**	To open the Check Spelling dialog box. You'll check the spelling for the illustration.
2 Click **Start**	Illustrator begins checking all the text in the document. It stops when it gets to the word "wildcrafted," which is not in the default English dictionary. This is a term specific to Outlander Spices, so you'll add it to the dictionary in case you encounter it again in future documents.
3 Click **Add**	Illustrator adds the word to the dictionary and continues with the spelling check. It stops again when it gets to the word "Cinamon," which is misspelled.
4 Observe the Suggestions pane	
	The correct spelling of the word "Cinnamon" is selected, which you'll use to fix the misspelling.
5 Click **Change**	Illustrator fixes the misspelling and continues with the spelling check. The dialog box now says "Spell Checker Complete," indicating there are no additional suspect words in the text.
6 Click **Done**	To close the dialog box. The word "Cinnamon" is selected in the text, which is the last word Illustrator corrected.
7 Deselect the text	
8 Update and close the document	And return to the My recipes_typography file.

Replace text

Explanation

At times, you might need to replace all occurrences of a word or a phrase in an illustration with another word or phrase. If the word or phrase appears multiple times, replacing it manually can be tedious and time-consuming. Instead, use the Find/Change command to search for and replace the specified text automatically. You can replace all occurrences, or you can replace text at selected instances. Either way, each replacement is made without changing any text attributes.

ACE objective 4.3

To find and replace text:

1 Choose Edit, Find and Replace to open the Find And Replace dialog box, shown in Exhibit 8-12.

2 In the Find box, enter the text you want to search for.

3 In the Replace With box, enter the replacement text.

4 Click Find to search for and select the first instance of the specified text.

5 To replace the text:

- Click Replace to replace only the current instance of the selected text.

- Click Replace & Find to replace the current instance of the selected text and find the next instance of the same text.

- Click Replace All to replace all instances of the selected text.

6 Click Done.

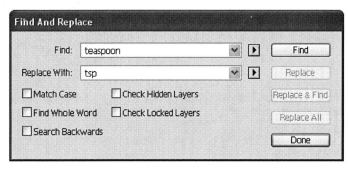

Exhibit 8-12: The Find And Replace dialog box

Do it!

C-2:   Finding and replacing text

ACE objective 4.3

Here's how	Here's why
1 Zoom in on the chicken recipe ingredients	(In the My recipes_typography document.) So that the text is clearly visible. In the list of ingredients for both recipes, you want to replace each instance of the word "teaspoons" with the shortened abbreviation "tsp."
2 Choose **Edit**, **Find and Replace...**	To open the Find and Replace dialog box.
3 In the Find box, enter **teaspoons**	
4 In the Replace box, enter **tsp**	
5 Click **Find**	Illustrator begins searching all the text in the document and stops at the first instance of the word "teaspoons."
6 Reposition the dialog box	If necessary, to see the first selected instance of the word "teaspoons" in the text.
7 Click **Replace**	To replace the word with the abbreviated version.
8 Click **Find Next**	Illustrator continues searching the text and stops at the next instance.
9 Click **Replace & Find**	To automatically replace the word and continue with the search.
10 Click **Replace All**	To automatically replace all instances of the word "teaspoons" with the abbreviated version. A dialog box appears, indicating that ten changes were made.
11 Click **OK**	To close the dialog box.
12 Click **Done**	To close the Find and Replace dialog box.
13 View the entire artboard, then deselect the text and update the document	

Font usage

Explanation

ACE objective 4.3

You might need to replace a font used in an illustration with a different font. For example, you might be updating an illustration you created a while ago, and you might be restricted to certain fonts that weren't used in the previous version. You also might have accidentally applied a font that you don't want used in the document.

To replace fonts in an illustration:

1   Choose Type, Find Font to open the Find Font dialog box, shown in Exhibit 8-13.

2   In the Fonts in Document section, select the font that you want to replace.

3   In the Replace With Fonts From section, select the font that you want to use to replace the original font, and set the desired options:

   - Choose an option from the Replace With Font From list: You can choose Document to list only the fonts that are used in the document or System to list all fonts on your computer.

   - At the bottom of the dialog box, check the kinds of fonts you want to include in the list or clear the kinds of fonts you don't want to include.

4   To change the font:

   - Click Change to change just one occurrence of the selected font.

   - Click Change All to change all occurrences of the selected font. When there are no more occurrences of a font in your document, its name is removed from the Fonts in Document list.

5   Click Done to close the dialog box.

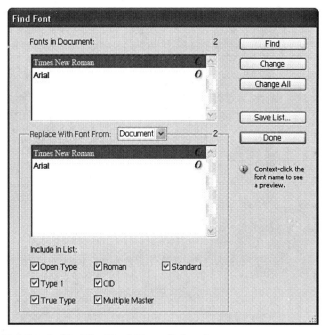

Exhibit 8-13: The Find Font dialog box

When you replace a font by using the Find Font command, all other type attributes remain the same.

Do it!

C-3: Managing font usage

Here's how	Here's why
1 Choose **Type, Find Font...**	To open the Find Font dialog box.
2 Observe the **Fonts in Document** pane	Fonts in Document: Times New Roman **Times New Roman Bold** **Arial Bold** Arial **Arial Black** The pane lists five font variations used in the text; each variation is either Times New Roman or Arial. However, you only want to use Arial in the text.
3 In the Fonts in Document list, select **Times New Roman Bold**	
4 Click **Find**	To view the text in the illustration that currently is formatted with Times New Roman. (You might need to reposition the dialog box to see the selected text.)
5 In the Replace With Font From pane, click **Arial Bold**	(If necessary.) To specify that you want to reformat the text with Arial Bold.
6 Click **Change**	To reformat the text with Arial Bold.
7 Click **Change All**	To automatically update any other text in the illustration formatted with Times New Roman Bold to Arial Bold.
8 In the Fonts in Document list, select **Times New Roman**	
9 Replace Times New Roman with Arial	Click Find, select Arial in the Replace With Font From list, and click Change All.
10 Observe the Fonts in Document pane	Fonts in Document: Arial Bold Arial **Arial Black** Times New Roman Bold no longer appears in the list.
11 Click **Done**	To close the Find Fonts dialog box.
12 Update and close the document	

Unit summary: Adjusting typography

Topic A   In this topic, you learned how to **flow type through linked type containers** and **wrap text** around items.

Topic B   In this topic, you learned how to **set and format tabs, insert typographic characters,** and **use character and paragraph styles**.

Topic C   In this topic, you learned how to **check spelling, find and replace text** in a document, and **manage fonts**.

Independent practice activity

In this activity, you'll import text from a Word document into a type container. You'll then link the text to other type containers so that all the text is visible. You'll then wrap some of the text around an image of a plate of food. Lastly, you'll format and update some of the text by means of spell checking and font usage.

1   Open the Princely potatoes_typesetting practice document (located in the current unit folder). Save the document as My princely potatoes_typesetting practice.

2   Import the Potatoes text_practice Word document so that the text is inside the white rectangle near the top of the illustration.

3   Link the type container to the white rectangle near the bottom of the illustration, similar to the example in Exhibit 8-14. (*Hint*: Use the Selection tool to click the red plus port at the bottom of the type container. Position the pointer on one of the edges of the lower white rectangle, and click to convert the rectangle to a linked type container.)

4   Bring the small image of the plate of food to the front of the stacking order; then create a text wrap so that the ingredients for the potatoes recipe flow around the right side of the plate, similar to the example in Exhibit 8-15. (*Hint*: With the image selected, choose Object, Text Wrap, Make.)

5   Readjust the size of the type container at the top of the illustration so that all of the ingredients are visible. Format the ingredients text white, but leave the directions text in the bottom type container black, similar to the example in Exhibit 8-16.

6   Check the spelling for all the text in the document. Correct any misspellings. (*Hint*: Ignore any abbreviations such as "tbsp" if Illustrator flags them as suspect words.)

7   Change all instances of the word "teaspoons" in the text to the abbreviation **tsp**.

8   Readjust the size of the type container at the top of the illustration so only the ingredients are visible. All the Directions text should be in the lower type container.

9   Check the fonts used in the illustration. Change the fonts so that only Arial, Arial Bold, or Arial Black are used in the text. Replace any instances of Times New Roman Bold with Arial Bold. (*Hint*: Open the Find Font dialog box. In the Fonts in Document section, select Times New Roman Bold. In the Replace With Font From section, select Arial Bold.)

10   Update and close the document.

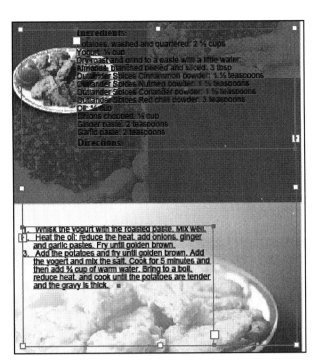

Exhibit 8-14: The illustration after completing step 4 in the Independent practice activity

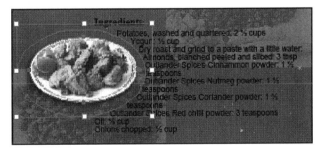

Exhibit 8-15: The illustration after completing step 5 in the Independent practice activity

Exhibit 8-16: The illustration after completing step 6 in the Independent practice activity

Review questions

1 How can you insert a special character into text?

A Choose Type, Insert, and select the special character you want from the available list.

B Choose Window, Type, Glyphs to open the Glyphs panel, and then double-click the special character you want to add.

C Choose Window, Type, Character to open the Character panel, and then double-click the special character you want to add.

D Choose Type, Show Hidden Characters, and select the special character you want from the available list.

2 What expanded capabilities do OpenType fonts provide? (Select all that apply.)

A A larger selection of ligatures, swashes, and old-style proportional figures.

B A single font file for both Macintosh and Windows computers.

C Editable outlined text.

D Superscript and subscript characters.

3 Which statements about character and paragraph styles are true? (Select all that apply.)

    A Character styles affect only selected portions of text; paragraph styles affect entire paragraphs.

    B Character styles include only basic character formatting options such as font styles and font color; paragraph styles include character formatting in addition to paragraph formatting, such as indent settings and text alignment options.

    C Character styles include only basic character formatting options such as font styles and font color; paragraph styles include only paragraph formatting and cannot include character formatting.

    D Character styles affect entire paragraphs of text; paragraph styles affect only selected portions of text.

4 You are using the Tab panel to position tab markers for text in an illustration. What are ways you can position a tab marker where you want it? (Select all that apply.)

    A Drag the tab marker in the tab ruler.

    B Enter a value in the Leader box.

    C Select a tab marker type in the Tabs panel; then click where you want the tab at the top of the type container.

    D Enter a value in the Tab Position box.

5 You've imported text into a type container. However, the type container is not large enough, and a red plus sign indicates there is overflow text. How can you link the type container to another type container so all the text is visible?

    A Right-click the type container containing the text and choose Link, Link Type Container; then click on the type container you want to link to.

    B Double-click the type container containing the text, and then click on the type container you want to link to.

    C Using the Selection tool, click the port containing the red plus sign on the type container containing the text, and then click on the type container you want to link to.

    D Press and hold Alt; then drag from the port containing the red plus sign on the type container containing the text to the type container you want to link to.

6 You have text in a type container that you want to wrap around the outside of an image. How can you wrap the text around the image?

    A Position the text so that it overlaps the image, select the text, and choose Object, Text Wrap, Make.

    B Position the image so that it overlaps the text, and then right-click the image and choose Create Text Wrap.

    C Position the text so that it overlaps the image, and then right-click the image and choose Create Text Wrap.

    D Position the image so that it overlaps the text, and then select the image and choose Object, Text Wrap, Make.

7 You have opened the Find Font dialog box, and notice that Times New Roman is listed as being used somewhere in the illustration. However, you want to use Arial only. How can you change each instance of Times New Roman to Arial?

A In the Fonts in Document section, select Arial. In the Replace With Fonts From section, select Times New Roman. Then click either Change or Change All.

B In the Fonts in Document section, select Times New Roman. In the Replace With Fonts From section, select Arial. Then click either Change or Change All.

C In the Fonts in Document section, right-click Times New Roman and choose Arial from the list of fonts.

D In the Fonts in Document section, right-click Arial and choose Times New Roman from the list of fonts.

8 You are using the Check Spelling command to check the spelling for text in an illustration. How can you correct the spelling for any suspect words? Select all that apply.

A Select the correctly spelled word in the Suggestions box, and then click Change.

B Activate the type container containing the highlighted suspect word, and then type the correct spelling in the text.

C Type the correct spelling for the word in the Word Not Found box, and then click Change.

D Right-click the suspect word in the Word Not Found box, and then select the correctly spelled word from the list of suggestions.

Appendix A

ACE exam objectives map

This appendix provides the following information:

A ACE exam objectives for Illustrator CS3 with references to corresponding coverage in ILT Series courseware.

Topic A: ACE exam objectives

Explanation The following table lists the Adobe Certified Expert (ACE) exam objectives for Adobe Illustrator CS3 and indicates where each objective is covered in conceptual explanations, hands-on activities, or both.

#	Objective	Course level	Conceptual information	Supporting activities
1.0	**Laying out a document**			
1.1	Describe the different components of the work area. (Components include: Artboard, Page area, Panels, and Tools.)	Basic	Unit 1, Topic A	A1, A2, A3
1.2	Explain how to use grids, guides, and rulers.	Basic	Unit 2, Topic B	B2
1.3	Given a scenario, select and configure the appropriate settings in the Document Setup dialog box.	Basic	Unit 2, Topic A	A2
1.4	Given a scenario, select the appropriate New Document preset. (Scenarios include: Print, web, and mobile documents)	Basic	Unit 2, Topic A	
2.0	**Working with shapes and objects**			
2.1	Given a tool, create an object. (Tools include: Pen, shape tools, and Pathfinder)	Basic	Unit 2, Topic B Unit 4, Topic B Unit 4, Topic C	B1 B2, B3, B4 C1
2.2	Given a scenario, choose the appropriate tool to select an object or the points of an object. (Scenarios or tools include: Selection tool, Direct Selection tool, Isolation mode, Select menu commands)	Basic Advanced	Unit 2, Topic C Unit 4, Topic C Unit 3, Topic A	C1, C5 C1
2.3	Given a scenario, transform objects. (Scenarios include: Rotate, reflect, and scale an object; Transform Again; Align (Align to Artboard, Align to Crop, Align and Distribute Points))	Basic Advanced	Unit 2, Topic C Unit 1, Topic A Unit 3, Topic A	C1, C3, C6, C7 A6 A2, A3
2.4	Given a command or tool, distort an object. (Commands or tools include: Warp tools, mesh tools, and Envelope Distort)	Advanced	Unit 3, Topic B Unit 3 Topic C	C1
2.5	Given a scenario, edit the stroke and/or fill attributes of an object. (Scenarios include: stroke alignment, overprinting, and dash patterns)	Basic	Unit 3, Topic B	B1, B2

#	Objective	Course level	Conceptual information	Supporting activities
2.6	Control the appearance of an object by using the Appearance panel. (Situations include: Applying multiple strokes and/or fills, clearing and setting basic appearance)	Advanced	Unit 2, Topic A	A1
2.7	List and describe the differences between filters and effects.	Advanced	Unit 4, Topic A	
2.8	Select the appropriate settings, and convert a bitmap file to vector artwork by using the Live Trace command.	Advanced	Unit 5, Topic A	A1, A2
2.9	Create and color artwork by using the Live Paint tools.	Advanced	Unit 5, Topic B	B1, B2
2.10	Create and modify masks, including clipping masks.	Advanced	Unit 1, Topic B	B1, B2
2.11	Create, use, and customize brushes.	Advanced	Unit 2, Topic E	E1, E2, E3
2.12	Modify overlapping objects by using the Transparency panel.	Basic	Unit 7, Topic C	C1
2.13	Change the appearance of objects by using the Graphic Styles panel.	Advanced	Unit 4, Topic C	C1
2.14	Create, use, and edit symbols by using the Symbols panel and Symbols tools.	Advanced	Unit 2, Topic F	F1
2.15	Create and modify compound shapes by using Pathfinder panel or the Eraser tool.	Basic	Unit 2, Topic C	C4
		Advanced	Unit 1, Topic A	A4, A5
2.16	Apply Photoshop filters and effects to artwork.	Advanced	Unit 4, Topic A Unit 4, Topic B	A2 B3

3.0   Working with color

#	Objective	Course level	Conceptual information	Supporting activities
3.1	Create spot colors and add them to the Swatches panel.	Basic	Unit 7, Topic A	A2
3.2	Apply colors, strokes, fills, and gradients to objects by using the Fill box, Stroke box, or Appearance panel.	Basic	Unit 3, Topic A	A1, A2
		Advanced	Unit 2, Topic A	A1
3.3	List and describe the functionality of the Color Guide panel. (Functionality includes: color harmony rules, panel options, color groups)	Basic	Unit 3, Topic A	
3.4	Recolor artwork by using the Live Color dialog box.	Advanced	Unit 2, Topic B	B3

#	Objective	Course level	Conceptual information	Supporting activities
4.0	**Working with type**			
4.1	List and describe the advantages and disadvantages when using OpenType, True-Type, or Type 1 fonts.	Basic	Unit 8, Topic B	
4.2	Add type to a document.	Basic	Unit 5, Topic A	A1, A2
4.3	Manage the composition of text by using panels, menus, and preferences settings.	Basic	Unit 5, Topic A Unit 8, Topic B Unit 8, Topic C	A1 B1 C1, C2, C3
4.4	Create and modify type by using Character and Paragraph styles.	Basic	Unit 8, Topic B	B3, B4
4.5	Create outlines of type by using the Create Outlines command.	Basic	Unit 5, Topic B	B3
4.6	Change the look of type by using the Envelope commands.	Advanced	Unit 3, Topic B	B1, B2
4.7	Insert special characters by using the Type menu and the Glyphs panel.	Basic	Unit 8, Topic B	B2
4.8	Given a scenario, choose the appropriate option for dealing with legacy text. (Scenarios include: open file and update all legacy text, update all, update one, exporting to legacy Illustrator versions)	Basic	Unit 8, Topic A	A2
5.0	**Managing color**			
5.1	Discuss the color management workflow process that is used in Adobe Illustrator.	Advanced	Unit 6, Topic A	
5.2	Set up color management in Illustrator by using the Color Settings dialog box.	Advanced	Unit 6, Topic A	A1
6.0	**Managing assets with Bridge**			
6.1	List and describe the functionality Adobe Bridge provides for viewing assets.	Basic	Unit 1, Topic A	A4
6.2	Explain how to apply metadata and keywords to assets in Adobe Bridge.	Basic	Unit 2, Topic D	D2
6.3	List and describe the functionality and set the appropriate options for Creative Suite Color Settings.	Advanced	Unit 6, Topic A	A2

#	Objective	Course level	Conceptual information	Supporting activities
7.0	**Outputting to print**			
7.1	Prepare and output a document to be used for color separation.	Advanced	Unit 6, Topic C	C1
7.2	List and describe the options available for previewing output and resolving common printing problems by using Overprint Preview, Flattener Preview, Live Color, and Transparency Flattener presets.	Advanced	Unit 6, Topic B	
7.3	Prepare a document for printing by choosing and configuring the appropriate resolution and rasterization settings.	Basic Advanced	Unit 2, Topic A Unit 6, Topic B	
7.4	Explain guidelines associated with printing gradient mesh objects and color blends.	Advanced	Unit 6, Topic B	
7.5	Given a scenario, use the Crop Area tool to modify output. (Scenarios include: cropping to a portion of the artwork, creating multiple crop areas, switching between crop areas)	Advanced	Unit 6, Topic B	B1, B2
8.0	**Saving and exporting**			
8.1	Given a file type, describe the options available when exporting an Illustrator document to that file type.	Basic	Unit 2, Topic D	D3
8.2	List and describe the options available for saving Illustrator documents by using the Illustrator Legacy Options dialog box.	Basic	Unit 2, Topic A	
8.3	Describe the differences, and explain criteria for when you would output an Illustrator document to various file formats. (formats include: PSD, EPS, PDF, SVG)	Basic	Unit 2, Topic D	D3
9.0	**Publishing for the Web**			
9.1	Discuss options and considerations associated with preparing graphics that will be used on the Web.	Advanced	Unit 7, Topic A Unit 7, Topic B	
9.2	Export Illustrator images that are optimized for publication on the Web.	Advanced	Unit 7, Topic B	B1, B2
9.3	Given a scenario, output artwork to the SWF format. (Scenarios include: Save for Web and Exporting.)	Advanced	Unit 7, Topic B	B4
9.4	Explain how to preview content for a mobile device by using Device Central.	Advanced	Unit 7, Topic B	

Course summary

This summary contains information to help you bring the course to a successful conclusion. Using this information, you will be able to:

A Use the summary text to reinforce what students have learned in class.

B Direct students to the next courses in this series (if any), and to any other resources that might help students continue to learn about Adobe Illustrator CS3.

Topic A: Course summary

At the end of the class, use the following summary text to reinforce what students have learned. It is intended not as a script, but rather as a starting point.

Unit summaries

Unit 1

In this unit, students learned how to **start Illustrator**, and explored the **Illustrator environment**. Students opened files with both Illustrator and **Adobe Bridge**. They also learned how to **navigate** an Illustrator document. Finally, they used the **Adobe Help Viewer** to search for help in using Illustrator.

Unit 2

In this unit, students learned how to **create and save a new document**. They learned how to **draw basic shapes** using some of the **shape tools**, and students learned to **manipulate shapes as they draw them**. Students also learned how to **draw shapes precisely**. Students learned how to **manipulate existing shapes**. This included **scaling, rotating, aligning, and distributing shapes**. Students also learned how to **combine simple shapes to make a compound shape**. Lastly, they learned how to **add metadata** to files and to **export an illustration** to several common formats.

Unit 3

In this unit, students **adjusted the fill and stroke colors** for shapes. They **applied color** using the **Swatches panel** and the **Color panel**, and students **stored custom colors in the Swatches panel**. Students **applied stroke color** to shapes and **adjusted the thickness of a stroke**. They also created a **dashed stroke**. Lastly, they **used the Eyedropper tool** to quickly sample fill and stroke attributes and apply them to other shapes.

Unit 4

In this unit, students learned how to **link or embed raster graphics** in an Illustrator file. Students learned how to draw shapes and paths by **using the basic drawing tools**. They created freeform shapes by using **the Pencil tool** and created more precise paths using **the Pen tool**. They learned how to select and edit paths, including manipulating anchor points, by using the **Add Anchor Point, Delete Anchor Point, and Convert Anchor point tools**, as well as cutting paths by using the **Scissor and Knife tools**. Lastly, students joined open paths by using the **Average and Join commands**.

Unit 5

In this unit, students learned to use **the Type and Vertical Type tools** to add text to an illustration. They also learned how to **import text from an external document** and format text by using **the Character and Paragraph panels**. Students learned to creatively alter text. Students **inserted text into custom shapes, positioned text on a path**, and **converted type to outlines**.

Unit 6

In this unit, students learned to **create new layers and reassign items to them**. They also learned to **adjust the stacking order for layers**, and to **lock layers** and **adjust their visibility**. Students learned to **manipulate layers by renaming sublayers, duplicating layers**, and **deleting layers**.

Unit 7

In this unit, students learned to **import swatch libraries** from other documents, **open preset swatch libraries**, and **export colors in the Swatches panel** as a new custom library. They learned to **create and apply gradients** to items in an illustration. They also **adjusted a gradient** by changing its angle and applying it evenly to multiple shapes. Students learned to **adjust the opacity for an item** by using the Transparency panel. This included **applying a blending mode** so that the color of underlying items mixed with the overlapping items.

Unit 8

In this unit, students learned how to **flow type through linked type containers** and **wrap text** around items. They also learned how to **set and format tabs, insert typographic characters**, and **use character and paragraph styles**. Lastly, they learned how to **check spelling, find and replace text** in a document, and **manage fonts**.

Topic B: Continued learning after class

Point out to your students that it is impossible to learn to use any software effectively in a single day. To get the most out of this class, students should begin working with Adobe Illustrator CS3 to perform real tasks as soon as possible. We also offer resources for continued learning.

Next courses in this series

This is the first course in this series. The next course in this series is:

- *Illustrator CS3: Advanced, ACE Edition*

Other resources

For more information, visit www.axzopress.com.

Illustrator CS3: Basic

Quick reference

Button	Shortcut keys	Function
	CTRL + O	File, Open
	CTRL + S	File, Save
	CTRL + W	File, Close
	CTRL + Y	Switches between Outline and Preview modes
	TAB	Hide/Show all open palettes
	SHIFT + TAB	Hide/Show all open palettes except the toolbox
	CTRL + "	Show/Hide grid
	F1	Opens the Adobe Help Center window
(Hand tool)	SPACEBAR	Moves the Illustrator artboard within the illustration window (Pressing the Spacebar temporarily accesses the Hand tool when you are using a different tool.)
(Zoom tool)	Z	To select the Zoom tool
(Zoom out tool)	(Zoom) + ALT	Click to zoom in
	CTRL + +	Zoom in
	CTRL + –	Zoom out
	CTRL + SHIFT +]	Brings a selected object to the front of the stacking order
	CTRL + SHIFT + [	Sends a selected object to the back of the stacking order
	CTRL + 0 (zero)	Changes the document magnification so that the artboard fits within the application window
	CTRL + 1	Changes the document magnification so that the artwork appears at actual size

Glossary

Adobe Bridge

A helper application for managing documents and Adobe Creative Suite projects.

Anchor points

Points along a vector path through which the path flows, much like the dots in a connect-the-dots drawing.

Artboard

The area of the illustration that will be printed. The artboard can be smaller or larger than the current page size.

Cap

The shape at the end of a stroke. Options include squared off ends (butt and projecting) and rounded caps.

Clipping mask

A vector path that frames other objects so those objects are visible only within the clipping mask.

Closed path

A series of straight or curved lines in which the start and end points meet, making it a closed shape.

Control panel

A panel, usually at the top or bottom of the Illustrator window, that displays options based on the selected item.

Corner point

An anchor point on a vector path in which the two segments flow in different directions. The direction points for a corner point don't have to face exactly opposite one another.

CMYK color

A color defined by Cyan, Magenta, Yellow, and Black components, typically used for commercial printing.

Color model

The method of defining colors based on component values. For example, the RGB color model defines colors by their Red, Green, and Blue components, whereas the CMYK color model breaks colors into Cyan, Magenta, Yellow, and Black components.

Compound shape

A shape in which two or more shapes are partially combined to act as one shape, but can still be individually manipulated.

Direction point

A point extending from an anchor point on a vector path that determines the curvature of the adjoining segment.

Embedded image

A raster image that is stored within an Illustrator document.

Fill

The color, pattern, or gradient of the area within the outline of a shape or path.

Gradient

A blend of two or more colors in which the colors fade gradually from one to another.

Join

The shape of a stroke at a corner point. Options include mitered, rounded, and beveled joins.

Layer

An item in the Layers panel that acts much like a stacked transparent sheet that can contain items, groups, and other layers. You can hide layers, adjust their stacking order, and select all of the items on a layer.

Linked image

A raster image that appears within artwork but which is actually an external file referenced by the Illustrator document, not stored within it.

Metadata

Information stored along with a file, typically with descriptive keywords and data about the document's source and purpose.

Open path

A series of straight or curved lines in which the start and end points do not meet.

Panel

A small window that floats above the document window and helps you monitor, arrange, and modify artwork.

Pasteboard

The nonprintable areas outside the artboard which you can use for rough work you want to store but don't intend to print.

Path

A geometric shape such as a smoothly flowing curve, defined by a series of points with segments between them (as opposed to a grid of pixels, as in a raster image).

Raster image

An image comprised of a grid, or raster, of pixels.

RGB color

A color defined by Red, Green, and Blue components, typically used for Web graphics and inkjet printing.

Segment

The part of a vector path between two anchor points.

Smooth point

An anchor point on a vector path in which the segments on either side curve in the same direction. Smooth points have direction points that face exactly opposite one another.

Spot color

A color that is printed with a single pre-mixed ink.

Status shortcut menu

A menu at the bottom of the Illustrator window that can display information such as the current tool, available memory, and available number of undos.

Stroke

The outline of a shape or path, which can be a solid or dashed line.

Swatch

A saved color, gradient, or pattern that you can apply to artwork via the Swatches panel.

Tools panel

The panel containing tools you use to draw and edit in your document.

Vector graphic

An graphic created from mathematically defined paths, much like a connect-the-dots drawing with curvature allowed between dots.

Workspace

A saved arrangement of panels.

Zoom box

A box at the bottom of the Illustrator window with which you can view and change the magnification of the illustration.

Index